JOURNAL
OF A POLITICAL EXILE
IN AUSTRALIA

JOURNAL

d'un Exile Politique aux Terres

AUSTRALES

PAR

L. DUCHARME.

IMPRIME' PAR

F. CINQ-MARS,

BUREAU DE L'AURORE, RUE ST. AMABLE,

MONTREAL.

1845.

JOURNAL OF A POLITICAL EXILE IN AUSTRALIA

BY

Leon (Léandre) Ducharme

TRANSLATED AND INTRODUCED BY

George Mackaness

ETT IMPRINT
SYDNEY-PARIS LINK

This edition published by ETT Imprint, Exile Bay 2020.

First published by Australian Historical Monographs in 1944.
Reprinted from 1976 by Review Publications, Dubbo.

ETT IMPRINT
PO Box R1906
Royal Exchange NSW 1225
Australia

ISBN 978-0-922384-13-3 (paper)
ISBN 978-0-922384-19-5 (ebook)

A Sydney-Paris Link publication
in memory of Jean-Paul Delamotte

Cover: *Les Insurgés, à Beauharnois, Bas-Canada*,
by Katharine Jane Ellice, 1838
Cover design by Tom Thompson
Text design by Hanna Gotlieb

To Mrs. Dora Hood,
Toronto, Canada

Battle of Saint-Eustache by Charles Beauclerk.

CONTENTS

INTRODUCTION

The Rebellion in Lower Canada, 1837-1838.

The real cause of the trouble which brought about the two rebellions in Lower Canada in the years 1837-1838 was the sudden liberty which the French element received under the Constitutional Act of 1791, one which gave to both Provinces, Upper and Lower Canada, the right of the franchise and an elective Parliament, the British Government undoubtedly feeling that the best step would be to give the fullest civil government to all its subjects in Canada.

There was no general demand on the part of the French for a popular Assembly. They had never heard of such a thing during the one Hundred and fifty years of French rule, and felt no need of it. Though a few had petitioned for it, the great majority of the inhabitants were wholly satisfied to be allowed to practise their religion and to cultivate their fields without hindrance, But in the early part of the century certain French leader's, anti-British in spirit and attitude, began to throw their influence and the weight of the ballot box towards the creation of a faction actively opposed to British rule.

The British Government's vacillating policy contributed largely to the revolt. They tried in turn coercion and conciliation, thus weakening immensely their strength and influence over the French. Then, too, the British leaders had the fear that the French Province might break away and seek annexation with the United States. The trouble in Lower Canada consequently was largely due to British blunders, the principal of which was the conferring of the franchise inopportunely upon the inhabitants without restriction, when nine-tenths of them were unable to read to write and had no conception of what democracy meant.[1]

The French rebels and factionaries, under the leadership of Louis J, Papineau,[2] Speaker of the Assembly of Lower Canada since 1815, became obsessed with the thought of an independent nation with Papineau as its first President, believing that, having wrung many concessions from the British Government, if they blustered enough, it would yield Lower Canada independence.

The situation had become critical when Lord Melbourne, the Prime Minister, in an effort to discover the fundamental causes of the trouble, sent out a Parliamentary Commission of three - the Earl of Gosford, Sir, Charles Grey and Sir Georgle Gipps - to study the question. Gosford was appointed Governor-General as well as Commissioner.

Gosford tried his best to conciliate the French people, but by his liberal policy and many concessions confirmed the impression of British weakness. This played into the hands of Papineau and his party, who, growing bolder, were beginning to demand the impossible. They were helped, too, by the attitude of certain sympathetic members of the Imperial Parliament, including Sir William Molesworth and David Hume. More and more defiant resolutions were passed by the Assembly, the Supply Bill was rejected, and on 21st March, 1837, Gosford prorogued Parliament with nothing to show in his favour.

During the interval between Parliaments the Papineau party kept up its propaganda, scattering the seeds of insurrection into every hamlet and parish of the colony. Parliament met again on 2nd September. By this time the British section was well aroused. So was Gosford, who, finding it was impossible to do any business with the Assembly, again prorogued Parliament. In the meantime Grey and Gipps, who had returned to England, presented, with Gosford's approval, a Report, the sum and substance of which was that if Britain wished to keep Canada British she must act at once. The Imperial Parliament, by an overwhelming majority, then carried resolutions declaring the Canadian Council appointive, and giving authority to the Government at Quebec to take the necessary measures to secure order in the colony.

Papineau and his party, furious at this news, convened meetings in all parts of the colony exciting the people to rebellion. In every parish arose the cries, "Vive Papineau," "Vive la Nation Canadienne." In determined opposition, the British elements held similar gatherings. Clashes were inevitable.

The last Parliament of Lower Canada met on the 18th August, 1837, and lasted exactly eight days, being prorogued after having again refused Supply. The French element, irritated, began to turn their organizations, called "Patriotes," into military formations. Everywhere could be seen bodies of men drilling on British soil to overturn British government.

Gosford, believing insurrection inevitable, secured permission to instruct Sir John Colborne, who had just ended his term as Governor of Upper Canada, to return to Quebec to take command of the military force of the colony. At that time there were only 2000 soldiers in the garrison, all the equipment being rusted and out of date. Papineau and his assistant, Dr. Wolfred Nelson, an Englishman, organized mobs which paraded the streets of Montreal, shouting defiance of Britain, and venting their inflammatory doctrines in song and speech.

On 6th November the first clash between the French and the British elements took place, a small party of the latter being attacked by the "Sons of Liberty," the French organization. As a result of this clash, the Governor-General set up a Provisional Government for Montreal and dismissed a number of magistrates. Some of the hamlets began to take up arms; Sir John Colborne moved his headquarters to Montreal; Upper Canada offered its help; warrants were issued for the arrest of Papineau and others, who fled to the interior, there to carry on their activities. All along the Richelieu River rebel camps were organized, especially at St. Denis. Sporadic engagements soon took place. At St. Denis, Nelson, Papineau and O'Callaghan, editor of the French newspaper *Vindicator,* came into contact with a small force under Colonel Gore's command. Papineau and O'Callaghan lost their nerve, deserted their followers and fled to the United States. Colonel Wetheral badly defeated the rebels at St. Charles, the latter losing fifty-eight men killed.

On 5th December, 1837, martial law was proclaimed in the district of Montreal and large rewards offered for the capture of Papineau and others, Some American sympathisers from Vermont who invaded the colony were promptly dispersed. Dr. Wolfred Nelson and many others were arrested, the gaols at Montreal being soon filled with the rebels.

The insurrection in the neighbouring villages was also promptly quelled. One unfortunate episode was the burning of the Church of St. Eustache, nine miles north-west of Montreal, when nearly one hundred men and women lost their lives. This was the end of what we might call the First Rebellion in Lower Canada, and also the end of the highly idealized and long-dreamt-of *"Nation Canadienne"*

Then came Lord Durham as Governor-General. He arrived in Canada on 28th May, 1838, to find the gaols overflowing with political prisoners. As his instructions were to temper justice with mercy, he granted the rebels a general amnestv, with only twenty-four exceptions. Eight of these were political prisoners who had confessed their guilt. These, including Wolfredd Nelson, were transported to the Bermudas during the Queen's pleasure. The remaining eighteen who had fled across the American border were forbidden to return to Canada under penalty of death.[3]

So much for the First Rebellion. Durham, for reasons not quite relevant to this Introduction, resigned after a few months in Canada, and had left the colony only two days when a second rebellion, that with which we in this volume are most concerned, broke out in Lower Canada. It was the result of a long course of agitation which had been carried on along the American border throughout the months of Lord Durham's regime.

As early as February, 1838, numbers of Canadian refugees had gathered in the towns on the American side of the boundary line in the neighbourhood of Lake Champlain, where they received much sympathy and encouragement from the Americans. A proclamation drawn up and signed by Robert Nelson, a brother of Wolfred Nelson, declared the independence of Canada under a provisional government, of which Nelson was President and Dr. Côté a member. There is a suggestion that Papineau was also implicated, but he soon called off.

On 28th February, 1838, Nelson and Côté made an abortive attempt to capture Montreal, but retreated across the border, there to be disarmed by the American troops under General Wool.

During the summer months plans for a fresh insurrection aroused the "Patriotes" who gathered at St. Ours, St. Charles, St. Michel, L' Arcadie, Châteauguay and Beauharnois. As, however, no American aid was forthcoming, many returned to their homes. At Napierville, the rebels' headquarters, a party of refugees Ied by Nelson and two French officers named Hindenlang and Touvrey, on 4th November, 1838, joined Dr. Côté, who had with him two or three hundred armed men. There Robert Nelson was proclaimed "President of the Republic of Lower Canada." Within three days a force of 2500 men had collected, armed chiefly with pitchforks and pikes.

On 5th November, a force of' four or five hundred men sent south by Nelson under the command of Côté to secure arms and ammunition from American sympathisers, met several companies of Loyalist militia at Lacolle, After half an hour's skirmish, the rebels fled across the border, leaving behind them eleven dead and many prisoners. The Loyalists lost only two men.

Nelson, hearing that Sir John Colborne was advancing on Napierville with a strong force of regulars and militia, fell back on Odell town with more than a thousand men, nearly all armed with muskets obtained from the United States. There they were soon put to flight by a company of Loyalists who had occupied the town. Robert Nelson, seeing the day was lost, turned tail and rode for the American border. The rebels left on the field more than fifty men dead and as many wounded

On the same day Sir James Colborne entered Napierville. On his approach the remaining rebels dispersed and fled, though a minor encounter took place, with some casualties, at Beauharnois, where the British soldiers, unfortunately, burnt down a large part of the village, including the homes of many of the "notorious rebels." The rebellion, which was hopeless from the start, had lasted scarcely a week.

As was the case in 1837, most of the leaders escaped from justice, leaving only the smaller fry in the hands of the authorities. Of these nearly one hundred were brought to trial.[4] Twelve of these, including the French, officer Hindenlang, were condemned to death and duly executed. As narrated in *Ducharme's Journal,* fifty-eight were transported to New South Wales. It is worthy of remark that none of those executed or deported had been persons of note in the political arena before 1837.

* * * *

Of contemporary accounts of the rebellion in Lower Canada, the two most important and interesting were both written by prisoners transported to New South Wales. The longer is *Notes d'un Condamné Politique de 1838*, by Francois Xavier Prieur, Montreal, 1864. Of this a new edition appeared in 1884. I published a translation in 1949. The other, of which a translation follows, is Ducharme's *Journal,* a volume of great rarity, for only three copies exist in Australia, one in the Mitchell Library, one in the collection of Mr. Justice J. A. Ferguson; and the third in my own possession.

NOTES

1. For a detailed account of the whole constitutional question, see *Cambridge History of the British. Empire,* Vol. Vl, chap, X, pp, 234 *et seq.*

2.Louis Joseph Papineau (1789·1871) worked his way to the head of the French-Canadian Party, and from 1815 to 1837 was Speaker of the House of Assembly for Lower Canada, and led the agitation against the Imperial Government. At the rebellion of 1837, a warrant was issued against him for high treason. He escaped to Paris, but returned to Canada, and was pardoned in 1847.

3. For the later political career of Papineau, see *Cambridge History of the British Empire,* Vol. VI., pp. 325, 334, 343, 340.

4. The complete and best account of the details of the rebellion will be found in *Report of the State Trials, Before a General Court Martial held at Montreal in* 1838-9, *exhibiting a Complete History of the Late Rebellion in Lower Canada.* Two volumes. Montreal,1839.

AUTHOR'S PREFACE

The public may perhaps have formed in advance an opinion much too favourable of the work that is now submitted to it. If it expects to read a Journal throbbing with interest, strewn with extraordinary incidents, narrated with all the graces of style, with every accomplishment that comes from a first-class education, then the author must begin by asking its pardon if it is disappointed in its expectations. The events, it is true, are set down there with the strictest accuracy, the most trifling incidents faithfully reported; but only the person who has experienced a protracted sea-voyage can understand the depressing sameness of the life that one leads there. The author, too, not having had, like so many others, the good fortune to receive a classical education, solicits the reader's indulgence for the style of his work. He feels, however, that this deficiency may make his journal doubly interesting. Nevertheless, he believes that the public will be grateful to him for any kind of narrative of the sufferings that his unfortunate fellow-exiles have undergone; and it is with this conviction that he has dared to publish the fruits of his observations set down day by day, persuaded that he might be excused much on the grounds of his good intentions.

At the same time, the author seizes the opportunity of renewing his thanks to His Excellency and to all those persons who were interested in his fate, as well as to each of his brothers in misfortune. He does not believe that he takes too much upon himself when he says that they all share his feelings, and that they have learned with much distress that they have been suspected of ingratitude. This suspicion should, of course, disappear when it is seen, in the course of this narrative, that as soon as they set foot on the American continent their very first thought was for their benefactors, and that, as far as they are concerned, it is a wholly inexplicable circumstance that this expression of their appreciation was not made public.

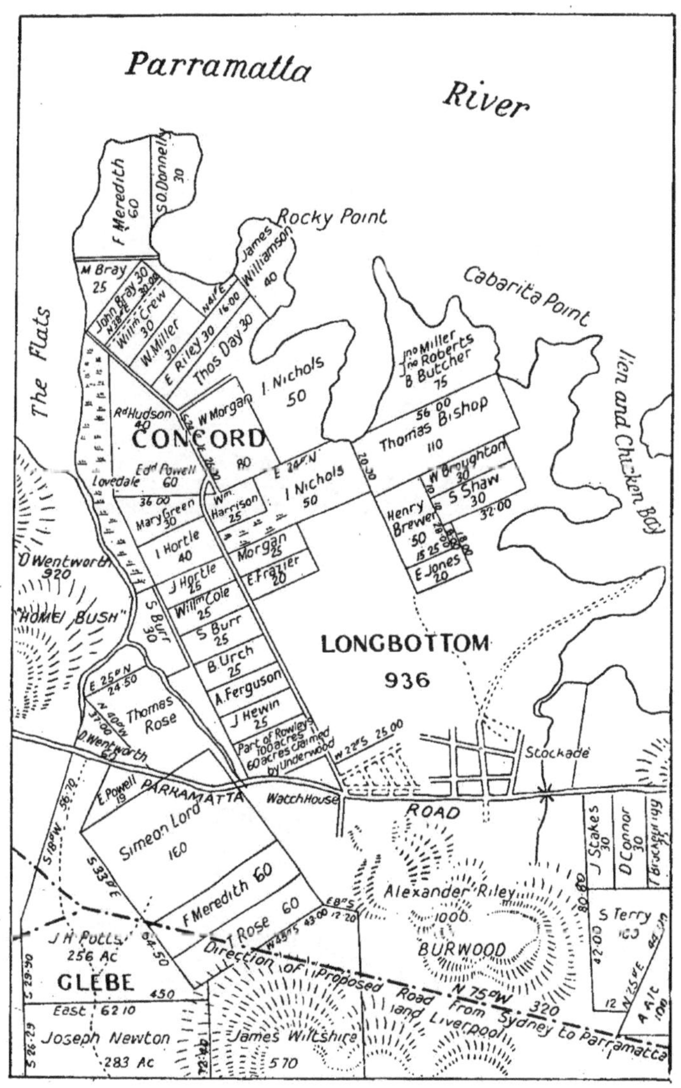

The Longbottom Stockade in Sydney's inner-west, as it was in 1840.

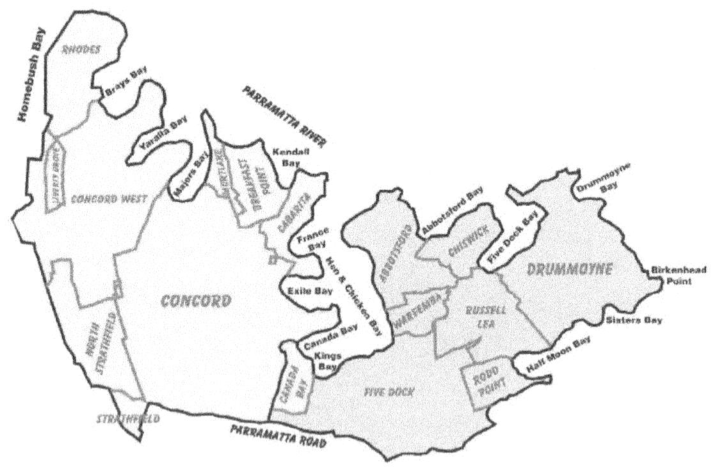

Sydney in 1843, by Frederick Garling.
A map of Sydney's inner-west, recognising the transported Patriotes of 1837, via the naming of Canada Bay, Exile Bay and France Bay.

JOURNAL

A Political in Exile

In November, 1838, together with a large number of Canadian rebels, I was arrested and lodged in the gaol at Montreal. I shall not attempt to give you the details of the insurrection, for these are sufficiently well known to you. I shall confine myself to an exact recital of our sufferings from the moment of our incarceration right up to the date of our return from exile to our own native land.

On the 24th of November, I received notice, conjointly with eleven others, to prepare myself to undergo my trial, which was set down for the 28th of the same month, before a Court-martial.

'We were at once separated from the other prisoners, and confined alone in one of the wards of the goal; as we were to appear before a tribunal quite exceptional in this country, we obtained permission to see two barristers, in order to consult with them about what we had to do, and to entrust them with our defence. I was amongst those who first underwent their trial before this Court-martial.

Our counsel filed an application to be supplied with a list of Judges of the Court who were to try us,' as well as one of the witnesses who were to testify against us; both requests were refused. Up to this time we had been able to communicate neither with our relatives nor our friends.

On the morning of the 21st, we were all chained together in pairs, and led before the Court, where, about an hour after our arrival, after having been thoroughly searched, we were freed from our fetters. The charges against us were then read out, and proceedings commenced.

At about five o'clock in the evening, the Court adjourned, and we were led away to La Pointe at Callières, under a strong escort of cavalry. It was midnight before we were released from the irons which secured us. The handcuffs of some of us were so small that they caused our wrists to become so swollen that they hid the irons which encircled them. The trial came to an end on the 14th December.[1] During the whole time it lasted, we were forced to remain standing before the Court, for we had no seats, having to support not only the weight of our bodies, but also that of the depositions of the Crown's witnesses. We were then taken back again to the goal at Montreal, where we remained separated from the others as before, while awaiting the result of our trial.

At last, after an interval of several days; at about, seven o 'clock one evening the cell-doors were opened, the roll called, and our sentences read to us. With the exception of two out of the twelve, we were all *condemned to be hanged.* We were then immediately locked up again in separate cells.' Every moment we awaited the order to prepare ourselves for mounting the scaffold. In fact, two days later Cardinal and Duquet[2] , two of our number, received the order to prepare for death on the following Friday. This was an ill-omen for us, since we believed that, for some reason or other, it had been decided to execute us a few at a time. I leave it to be judged what sort of situation we were in; however, we did not lack courage. Two days later we were witnesses of the heart-rending scene, for which; however, we too had to prepare ourselves. Our two unfortunate comrades, Cardinal and Duquet[2], manacled in our presence, were dragged out of the prison, with halters round their necks, led by the hangman...

We remained in the cells for thirty-three days, without being allowed out either day or night. We slept upon the bare floor, having only a single blanket both for bed and for covering, and this at a season of the year when frost covered the' whole interior of our cells.

When thirty-three days had passed, after much solicitation on our part we were permitted to open the doors of our cells for six hours each day, that is to say, from ten a 'clock until four; later, we obtained several additional hours, Such is the treatment experienced during our six months' imprisonment.

During this interval the dreadful scene of the execution of several among us was repeated several times. Those who underwent their trial after us were also treated in the same way.[3]

At last, on the 25th September, fifty-eight of us were warned to hold ourselves in readiness to go on board a steamer the following day bound for Quebec, and from there to embark on a vessel which would convey us to our destination, without, however, our being informed for how long we were to be exiled. On the 26th at four o'clock ill the afternoon, at low tide, we were chained, two by two, and taken on board the steamer *British America* under a strong escort of cavalry and infantry. As soon as we were in the open river, our chains were removed. We arrived at Quebec about eleven o'clock in the morning. While landing from the steamer and going on board H.M.S. *Buffalo,* our irons were again put on.

As soon as we were on board, we were again freed from irons, were sent below to the lower deck of the ship, and there locked up again. About seven o'clock in the evening, the prisoners from Upper Canada, to the number of eighty-three[4], joined us, and were lodged with us. We numbered then 141 in all; confined in quarters about forty feet long and approximately twenty-five feet wide. The whole centre was occupied by the hatches, the masts and the chains, the sides by our bunks which were ranged in a double row round the whole place, thus leaving only a small and very narrow alleyway through which we passed to go on deck and into the store-room to get our rations. Though the light could penetrate into this dungeon only through two hatchways, these were also stoutly barred.

On the 28th at six o'clock in the morning the anchor was raised, and we were towed by a steamer a few leagues below Quebec. The wind was favourable, the sails were unfurled, and we made our way down the Gulf with the help of a southwest wind. We had been divided into companies of twelve, and the regulations which we were to observe during the voyage were read out to us.

First, for breakfast we were issued about a pint of oatmeal porridge-which was brought to us in a pail containing the ration for twelve persons; at mid-day, we had, one day a half-pint of pea soup, a quarter of a pound of pork and about four ounces of biscuit; on the alternate day the same quantity of biscuit, three-quarters of a pound of salt beef, and about six ounces of *pudding* made from flour and a little lard; in the evening we were issued, one day a pint of tea only, the next a pint of chocolate. Such was our ration during the whole of the voyage; [5] these rations were issued to us in pails and we had only one tin plate, one knife, one fork and one spoon amongst twelve of us, Several of the prisoners not having provided ourselves with these utensils, thinking to find supplies of them on board, were compelled to tear with their teeth their meat which they held in one hand, while grasping their biscuit with the other, or else await their turn to use the knife and the fork.

As for the spoons, we succeeded in gumming together some little pieces of wood, out of which we made spoons or palettes which enabled us to eat our oatmeal soup. Our daily allowance of water was one pint each, a ration quite insufficient to quench the burning thirst brought about by the salty provisions. We were granted the pleasure of remaining on the top deck for two hours only each day. We went there in batches of thirty-six at a time so as to avoid overcrowding; this was the only time when we were able to have the pure fresh air. One-third of the main deck was allotted to us for exercise.

On the 30th September, the wind continued blowing violently from the south-west; we made very great progress; we had Cape Gaspé well in sight; we amused ourselves during our two hours' recreation watching countless numbers of dugongs which surrounded the ship. These are big fish, five or six feet long; which leap out of the water. We saw also two vessels at a short distance from us. Thus we made our way with the same breeze until the 2nd of October, when the wind blew with extraordinary force; the sea was in a fury; the waves rose to a prodigious height. Although I had often heard people talk of the sea, and read mariners' accounts, I confess that I was astounded to see such huge waves, and the ship poised in such a horrible manner. Those of us who were not tied down could neither stand nor sit. We continually collided with one another. In our dark quarters below we were tossed about from starboard to port without power to prevent it. Sea-sickness began to make itself felt, Three-quarters of us fell sick, and the number increased every minute, so that there remained only five or six who were not ill. In these circumstances nothing more affecting than our condition could be seen; salt provisions and biscuit were our only delicacies. For as long as four or five hours at a stretch several of us were unable to keep down even the slightest quantity of this food, and all of us were so weak that we were scarcely able to stand on our legs. In spite of this we were forbidden to lie down under threat of severe punishment, for exercise is necessary in treating this disease; but how could we stand erect when the vessel was tossed about by the waves, lying now on one side, now on the other?

We met an English brig called the *Queen Victoria,* upon which our pilot embarked to return to Quebec. The wind continued to blow with, the same violence until the month of October; during this time we were all very sick. The wind then began to decrease in force, and we directed our course South-East. We were then in the latitude of 55° 15' north. Oil this day we saw for the first time many flying-fish skimming the waves near the vessel. This attracted the attention of several of us, who, hitherto, had been sceptical regarding the existence of these fish. They are from eight to ten inches in length and fly only when the wind is blowing, for they direct their flight only with the wind; their numbers increased as we approached the equator, for they inhabit tropical regions only. Since we had come on board we had been made to wash the deck of our quarters every day and also to holystone it during the whole time we were passing from one tropic to the other. This was done to preserve the sweetness of the air about us. On the 11th, the weather became fine. The heat of the tropics already began to make itself felt, and caused us considerable distress. Our course was set steadily to the South-East. We caught sight of a Spanish ship in the East, travelling from this direction.

On the 12th we did not go on deck. We were kept at work the whole day washing and scrubbing our quarters. Just about five o'clock in the afternoon we were alarmed by the sound of firearms on deck, and by the coming and going of soldiers and crew, who in an instant were armed with guns, swords and pistols. We could not explain these movements. Then, some officers, coming down below with a squad of soldiers, compelled the whole 141 of us to go up to the between-decks, where we were packed into a space of about twenty-five feet square. There, without a word of explanation, they locked us up, and, after making us give up the keys of our boxes and trunks, went into our quarters, opened our trunks, some, with our keys, others with iron tools which forced off the lids. They searched all our clothes, took away our razors, our pocket knives our scissors and our money, with a little of which we had provided ourselves before our departure, they examined our beds, and all the chinks and crevices which might conceal any dangerous weapons. Finally, after searches as minute as they were useless, they came above to where we were; and one of the officers, whose name was Niblett, supported by several others, addressed us in the coarsest way, and told us that he had discovered the dark plot that we had formed to make ourselves masters of the crew, and to set a course for the shores of America: that he had crushed the conspiracy at its birth, and taken the necessary measures to forestall our ill designs. We tried to justify ourselves; we tried to assert that the idea of a mutiny against the crew had never come into our minds; that their the officers opinions could be founded only on false reports; that they should be convinced of this, by their searches of our quarters. We were compelled to be silent, even while being treated like dogs.

They made us go down below again, and drew up fresh regulations, severe and harsh. From this date, we were compelled to go to bed at eight o'clock precisely, and not to get up until six in the morning, except in case of urgent necessity; and even then it was necessary to give one's name to one of the sentinels who stood at our feet at certain intervals apart. So strictly was conversation forbidden amongst us that the sentinel had orders to shoot anyone who uttered a single word. From this time the officers came down below each evening at a quarter past eight with lanterns in their hands to ascertain whether we were all in our places and in bed. All the officers appeared to me to be extremely biassed against us, and exhibited a great deal of fear. Much of the space on deck which up till then we had enjoyed during our two hours recreation was now reduced.

In future we were forbidden to go on to the main deck; thus we were left with only about twenty feet along one half of the breadth of the ship in which to relax our limbs. The officers had, however, no cause for fear, since they were as numerous as we, soldiers as well as sailors, and all of them armed right down to the cook, who carried a sword and a pistol, and we were always under lock and key. Subsequently we discovered that a man named Tywell[6], one of the prisoners from Upper Canada, had spread this false report against his unfortunate companions, in the hope of being rewarded for his information by some mark of favour, or even by the recovery of his liberty. But when it came to be known amongst the crew how vile an imposter and a rogue he was, he was more detested and ill-treated on this account, both by them and by us. Nevertheless, the same severity continued to be employed towards us right up to the very moment of our disembarkation.

On the 13th and 14th, the wind blowing with great violence, we made nine knots an hour and on a set course, for we were steering so as to double the Cape of Good Hope.

On the 15th the breeze died down a little, but kept blowing in a direction favourable to us. The sun was blazing hot, and we suffered much from the heat in the between-decks where we were confined.

From the 16th to the 12th we experienced an almost continual calm. In this interval, one of our fellow-prisoners from Upper Canada, whose name was Priest,[7] who had come on board sick, died, partly from the effects of the ill-treatment he had received on board and partly through the lack of those comforts so necessary for a sick, man. As is customary, his body was sewn up in a sail-cloth to which four cannon balls were attached, and was cast into the sea in the presence of thirty-six of us. During the ceremony, the whole crew stood at attention under arms.

From the 21st to the 23rd we passed through the tropic (of Capricorn). During the course of these days, I had the distressing experience of seeing some of my companions ill-treated by a man named Black,[8] who, for certain crimes committed there, had been compelled to flee from Canada and to work his passage on board the *Buffalo.* He had been made our superintendent and, as is often the case, abused his authority so as to torment us, just as did the other man Niblett, whom I had occasion to mention a little while ago. Although we complained frequently to Captain Wood, commander of the ship, of the ill-treatment that his subordinates, possibly without his orders, made us undergo, he was always deaf to our complaints. Never did he come to see us, as every captain ought, to do, so as to find out whether we received such justice as that to which prisoners have the right; you can imagine then what our position was. In spite, however, of so many privations, I had the pleasure of seeing all my companions show themselves superior to all these trials, conforming courageously to all requirements, while hoping for happier days.

On the 24th, 25th and 26th, we had calm weather, with the exception of some light breezes which blew intermittently from the East. We then ran along the coast to Africa; the sea was covered with grasshoppers, and the air thick with them. The presence of these insects, of which we collected a great number on board, indicated to us that we were not very far from land. The sun was burning hot; no breath of air penetrated into the between-decks where we were; the heat there was suffocating, and, parched with thirst, we had only one pint of water each with which to quench it. What could this feeble remedy effect against a fire fed ceaselessly by our salt provisions? During these days, cotton shirts and cloth trousers provided by the Government were distributed amongst us. But, as we were not compelled to accept these garments, we rejected them almost in a body when we saw that they were branded. It was an ill omen for us. Only those amongst us who were the least provided with clothes, preserved their issue.

We were now in latitude north 18° 15". From the 27th to the 30th the wind blew violently. We saw swarms of flying fish. During the daytime of the 30th and the 31st we experienced several hurricanes, accompanied by rain, thunder and lightning, phenomena very frequent in these tropical regions and also very dangerous. In these localities it often happens that vessels are dismasted, for the storms are so sudden and so fierce that there is sometimes no time to take the necessary precautions. The masts are then carried away, the sails torn to ribbons, and despite of all precautions the ship cannot be prevented from being thrown on her side by the violence of the wind. But fortunately these spells of bad weather are only of very short duration.

The heat increased as we approached the Equator, and with it our sufferings; so much so that in the morning our mattresses, which were about three inches thick, were completely saturated with our sweat. To crown our sufferings, we were compelled to go to our beds at eight o'clock, and not to get up before six in the morning. During the day the majority of us could not bear to keep our shirts on, and our trousers were soaked through. We could not begin and conclude any task, so much were we in distress, for to the extreme heart of the air in our quarters, increased still more by that of our bodies and our breath, was added the most burning thirst.

From the 31st of October to the 5th of November we experienced calms and passing storms. Three of my companions were so ill during these latter days that we thought they were going to die. But they were restored by some boiled rice and tea that the ship's doctor obtained for them, We met a couple of ships on their way towards England - our captain entrusted some letters to one of them.

During the night of the fourth instant, there was an alarm on board, caused by one of the sentinels, who asserted that he had seen a light in the depths of our quarters. Then the whole guard at once went down below, under arms, and on arriving there they perceived that it was the light of a lamp from one of the hatches which reflected this pale gleam. They returned to the upper deck, crestfallen.

On the 5th November, convinced that the East-South-East wind would continue to blow steadily and contrary to our course, the captain determined to re-cross the Atlantic and pass along the coast of South America as far as Rio de Janeiro: There he expected to meet again the West and South-West winds known popularly as the trade winds, but scientifically as the "vents alizés" (regular winds) or monsoons. These are winds that blow regularly within the tropics and to some degrees beyond for six months in one direction and then six months in the other; that is to say, from the West from November to April, and from the East from April until November. We had two ships in sight, one Portuguese which was making for Brazil, and to which our captain spoke, the other English. We were now in latitude 20° North.

On the 5th at nine o'clock in the morning the heavens became covered with heavy clouds. An instant later there burst suddenly a frightful storm which lasted about two hours. Our sailors had had time to shorten sail; but that did not prevent the vessel from being badly tossed about. Some of the officers asked us if we were afraid; we replied that we were not, although some of us trembled with fright. Very soon the storm ceased.

On the 7th there was a heat wave, During the previous night a light breeze blew. The sea was now calm. Towards eight o'clock in the morning we crossed the Equinoctial Line, and found ourselves in the other hemisphere. This day was a holiday for our crew, as it is customary on all vessels when they make this passage. So we skirted the coast of South America. The heat was ever great; we could not stand upon the deck during our two hours of relaxation, for we had no shade to protect us from the scorching sun. The pitch ran everywhere. We had fierce gales accompanied by thunder and lightning. The breeze only came and went, and was followed by flat calm. On the deck of the ship were several long-boats, in which were confined pigs and sheep all covered with dung. After the storms, during which the rain usually fell in torrents, as much as eight or ten inches of water often accumulated in these boats. Well, the sailors hurried to fill bottles with this water, so impregnated with dung that it was brown in colour, and to us they sold it; sometimes we gave a shirt or a pair of trousers for one of these bottles, and such was the fierceness of our thirst that the water appeared to us as though it was honey.

In the between-decks we fitted hatches along the whole length of the iron gratings so that we could breathe a little fresh air.

On the 15th, while I was on deck there passed near us the masts of a ship, which probably indicated the misfortune of certain shipwrecked people in the neighbourhood. But, as the breeze was favourable, it was not thought necessary to undertake any search.

0n the 16th the breeze was strong. We noticed at a moderate distance the island of Fernandez. It is strange in appearance. High peaks in the form of columns rise to the clouds. This was a most striking object for us who had not seen land since our departure from the Gulf of St. Lawrence. However, it is just the same with all those who are at sea. We could not refrain from making certain reflections on our fate.

We were rapidly getting farther and farther away from our native land, without hope of ever seeing it again, and upon the vast ocean we were submitting to the decrees of Providence. Thousands of miles separated us from our fair land of Canada, from our families, our friends, all that was dear to us.

From the 17th to the 20th, the wind being moderate, we directed our course consistently towards the shores of Brazil. Our rate of sailing was three knots an hour.

On the 22nd the night was stormy, the breeze passably strong and favourable. The sailors caught a shark about eight feet long. These voracious fish are often seen at sea close to the ships, where they swallow all sorts of objects thrown overboard. In their stomachs have been found even such things as pieces of iron, a shoe and the shoulder-bone of an ox.

On the 23rd we had a strong north-west breeze, which lasted until the 26th. We were then in latitude 20° South.

On the 27th it was calm the whole day. As it was decided that we should call at Rio de Janeiro, we asked the captain for permission to buy some sugar and fruits with the same money which by his orders had been taken away from us -for in our present position we longed much for fruit as well as for every other kind of refreshing commodity. The captain sent us word that we could buy these things, and that we had only to make a note of all that we wished and he would procure them for us.

This news caused us great satisfaction.

At ten o'clock on the morning of the 28th we saw the shores of Brazil, which are very high. The sight of the land caused us to feel a lively sensation of pleasure, although, as far as freedom was concerned, we could hope for nothing. Nevertheless, this word *Land,* changed for so long into that of *Sea,* recalled to our mind sweet memories of our country. The joy that one experiences in such circumstances is inexpressible. The next day at six o'clock in the evening we arrived at the entrance to the Bay of Rio, but as the wind was contrary, we were compelled to remain in the open until the following day.

On the 30th at ten o'clock in the morning, with the help of a slight breeze, we entered and came to an anchorage before the town near some British frigates which were in the Port. Several officers came on board our ship to pay a visit to the captain; they came also to see us. A great number of boats loaded with fruits of all kinds came alongside. We bought a quantity for ourselves very cheaply. All the time that we were in the Port, instead of salt provisions, we were served with fresh meat and vegetables; this food appeared to us to be excellent, but it would have been better still if the quantity of it had been greater. During the time that we were at Rio, we were able, from the deck of the vessel to observe the town and its surroundings as well as the vast bay at the head of which the town is built. Two fine fortresses command the entrance to this Bay, which stretches away out of sight and is almost always full of shipping.

The town is built at the foot of high mountains which surround it. It has an air of antiquity about it. We were able to descry many magnificent edifices, amongst others being some Catholic Churches, for Catholicism dominates the Empire, where the population is Portuguese.

The houses have no chimneys, for the climate in the tropics dispenses with the necessity of maintaining a fire there. Cooking is carried on by means of stoves in the open air.

During the time that we were at Rio it was excessively hot, but the pleasure of seeing so many new objects made us able to put up with our disabilities.

On the 2nd of December was celebrated the anniversary of the Coronation of the Emperor of Brazil. He was fourteen years of age. The big guns of the fortresses and of all the warships then in port did not cease firing the whole day. In the evening the town was illuminated, and there was a grand display of fireworks.

At last, on the 5th of December, at six o'clock in the morning, we raised our anchor and put out to sea, setting our course for the Cape of Good Hope. We were favoured by a good westerly wind, which sent us along at the rate of seven or eight miles an hour; the heat which was so great at Rio began to diminish the farther we receded from the Equator. This same breeze carried us as far as 16°; during this time we were issued with the sugar and fruits that had been bought for us at

Rio; this did much to re-establish our health, which was considerably impaired as much by sea-sickness as by the bad food we received.

On the 17th a violent South-South-East wind blew up. The sky was covered with heavy clouds. The chill in the air began to make itself felt; several people even were constrained to put on their winter clothes.

During the course of the day a serious accident very nearly happened. One of the sentinels who used to mount guard in our quarters with a pistol in his hand, whether by chance or otherwise, caught the trigger while turning on one of the bars of the grating of the hatchway. The shot went through the centre of our quarters, and the bullet, in passing, entered the legs of one of the prisoners from Upper Canada and then lodged in a window-frame behind us. After some questioning by his superior officers, the sentinel was acquitted of blame.

From the 18th to the 27th the weather was calm. During these last days we had to endure Christmas Day, which caused us as much sadness and melancholy as it used to give us pleasure when we were in the midst of our families and friends. We had not yet lost the memory of those pleasant past times.

On the 28th we arrived on the same parallel as the Cape of Good Hope, driven by a westerly wind which blew with terrible force. The sea was so disturbed, and the ship so tossed about, that it was impossible for us to keep our feet or to remain seated without clinging desperately to some object. Never had we seen the sea so wild. You would have sworn that every minute the ship would have gone to the bottom; the waves pounded her so fiercely that she seemed to be hurling herself against a rock. The sea was quite white, and made a terrifying moan; the waves rose to a fearful height. This wind lasted until the 31st of December. During these last days we doubled the Cape where we should have called, if the wind had permitted. But as the place is difficult of access, it was resolved to pass it by. As far as we ourselves were concerned, we were not sorry. We were in such haste to be delivered from the distresses and all the other inconveniences that we were suffering on board that our one and only desire was to reach the land of our exile, believing that it was quite impossible to be more unhappy there than we were on board the ship.

On the 1st of January, 1840, thanks to the westerly wind which bowled us on, we were already well into the Indian Ocean, after having doubled the Cape of Good Hope. This day was still another one of sadness for us. How many memories does one not conjure up in moments like this! Our families, our friends, our pleasures, all come back into our imagination, and plunge us into a mood of depression, or a feeling of sadness that must be experienced to be understood; what contributed not a little to cast us into the depths of despair was the thought that all this was lost to us for ever...

From the 2nd until the 5th the wind blew with less violence; for two days we kept within sight of another vessel travelling in the same direction as ourselves.

On the 6th it rained the whole day. At two o'clock in the afternoon there blew up a squall which carried us along in the right direction at ten miles an hour.

From the 7th to the 11th the wind continued favourable with the exception of one whole day. We all suffered from distressing colds in the head caused by the humidity and the cold which already began to make itself felt.

The 12th was calm all day. It was the first calm day that we had experienced in the Indian Ocean.

From the 13th to the 14th the wind was moderate. I forgot earlier in the narrative to record that from the time of our embarkation there had been distributed amongst us, every fortnight, tobacco and pipes, of which we were permitted to make use during those two hours of relaxation on deck. We were told that this tobacco and these pipes had been put on board by some citizens of Montreal, for the use of the prisoners. The ship's authorities, with our consent, distributed some of them also to our fellow-prisoners from Upper Canada.

On the 15th, with fair weather and a fresh breeze, we passed within view of the Island of St. Paul, situated in the middle of the Indian Ocean. To us it appeared to be only a mountain peak. It is of very small extent and is not inhabited. We were told that it possesses two springs, of one of which the water is cold and wholesome, the other boiling. We knew that we were approaching some land by a multitude of sea-birds of great size which came flying around the ship.

On the 16th the wind, still favourable, became very much lighter. On the 17th it died away almost entirely.

On the 17th, the weather being fine, we had the pleasure of seeing the sailors and soldiers catch with a line some large birds called Albatross, which are very numerous in the Indian and Pacific Oceans. They caught some of them which had a width of from ten to seventeen feet, that is to say from wing-tip to wing-tip when fully spread out. This is the way the sailors capture them: They throw out a line of ordinary thickness with a fish-hook attached baited with a piece of meat. The bait, floating on the surface, drags behind the ship; sometimes they put it on a piece of cork to prevent it from sinking. As soon as the birds see the bait, they rush for it in dozens and seize it, only to find themselves caught by the beak. They allow themselves to be dragged along without making any resistance; on the contrary they help themselves by means of their wings to obey the hand which pulls them, for the greater their resistance the greater their suffering; and another strange thing is that as soon as they are on the ship they can be allowed to walk about freely on the deck without their making any attempt to flyaway. The flesh is not very good to eat; it has a slight fishy taste.

From the 19th to the 31st we had variable winds, and now and then rain. We saw also many whales round the ship. Our courage was renewed the closer we approached our destination. We met an American whaler on a whale-fishing cruise. We saw also schools of dugongs round the vessel.

On the 6th and 7th it blew a strong westerly wind, accompanied by rain. We are expecting very shortly to catch sight of the coast of Van Diemen's Land.

On the 8th, a strong wind and overcast weather. In the afternoon we caught sight of the expected Van Diemen's Land, which was the place where we were to disembark our companions in misfortune from Upper Canada. We coasted along the southern shores of this island, so as to enter the River Derwent, at the mouth of which is built Hobart Town, where we were to stay awhile.

On the 9th the wind came from the west and blew very hard, but in a direction contrary to that needed for our entry into the river. Towards noon it veered a little, so that we ran along the coast without much trouble. At eight o'clock in the evening we found ourselves near enough to the shore to distinguish the light of the candles and the fires of the dwellers on the coast. Suddenly the wind died away, and in the course of the night began to blow violently off-shore. We were driven out to sea so far that on the following day we could no longer see the land. We were so baffled by the winds that we were compelled to tack about a dozen times, without being able to reach the river mouth. It was not until the afternoon of this day that, the wind having changed a little, we easily entered the river, and about four o'clock in the afternoon dropped anchor before Hobart Town, principal town of Van Diemen's Land, There we remained for almost a fortnight without news of any kind. During this time, from the Port where we were anchored we could gaze upon the town and its surroundings. At last, on the fifteenth day, the prisoners from Upper Canada received notice to hold themselves in readiness to disembark the following day. And accordingly, at five o'clock on the next day, they disembarked to make their way ashore under no other escort than that of the men who had been sent to look after the sheep. We discovered that they had been sent about two miles from the township. They left us all in very good heart to take up their quarters at their penal establishment.

On the 10th and 17th we went up on deck as usual. We examined the town as well as we were able. To us it appeared somewhat rustic: a high mountain cuts off all the back country. Its buildings seemed to us fair enough, and the land on both sides of the River Derwent good and level. Some fields very well cultured were noticed. The port is very spacious, and is visited by many foreign ships, chiefly American and French whalers, who stop for provisions.

On the 18th we learned that the prisoners from Upper Canada were condemned for life; that they were to labour for the Government for a certain time only, and after that to be free within the land; that each one of them during the time of his servitude was to work at his trade for the benefit of the Government.

At six o'clock on the morning of the 19th the anchor was raised, and, favoured by a gentle breeze, we left the Bay. Towards eleven o 'clock, when we were in the open sea, a strong southerly wind sprang up, accompanied by a heavy downpour of rain. We were making fine headway in the direction of Sydney. Sails were crowded on, and this day a quick passage was made.

From the 20th to the 24th the wind blew with the same violence. It might have been said that Providence was anxious to hasten our arrival. We even began to talk already of arriving within a few days. We saw a ship heading for the west. On the 24th we discovered quite clearly the shores of New Holland, being continually favoured by a good southerly wind; for we had to direct our course to the north after leaving the River Derwent. At five o'clock we saw an English ship coming from London, of which both the captain and the chief officer had died during the journey. The cook was under suspicion of having poisoned them, and had been brought to trial at Hobart Town, where they had put into port. A boatswain had been compelled to take command of the vessel, which was loaded with emigrants for New South Wales.

On the morning of the 25th we again saw the coast, which appeared to us to be bordered by high mountains. But our view did not last long; the weather grew misty, and a thick fog developed which prevented us from seeing. The crew even feared for the ship's safety, for, as we were near the land we might encounter some reefs; we therefore put out again to the open sea. Towards ten o'clock the weather cleared, and once again we caught sight of the land. The coastline still appeared to us. very precipitous, and, the sea breaking upon it, the water rose up more than fifty feet into the air. About noon we caught sight of a lighthouse on a point dominating the shore; at the same time a pilot came on board, and we successfully entered Port Jackson and came to an anchor at Sydney Cove. So we arrived all safe and sound at our place of exile after a voyage of five months. It is astonishing to observe that so long and dangerous a voyage can he made without accident, even, though we had experienced bad weather that might have placed us in great danger. The crew themselves could not refrain from expressing their astonishment.

Although we knew that our new situation would not be very pleasant, we nevertheless experienced much pleasure at the thought that we had at last reached our destination. One must pass five long months at sea to understand how sweet it is to set one's foot on shore and to be free from the constraint of the ship.

On the 26th and 27th we came on deck as usual, and gazed with horror on this land that some few days previously we so ardently desired. Looking down from the deck we saw miserable wretches harnessed to carts, engaged in dragging blocks of stone for Public Buildings; others were breaking stones; the sight of this brought to us many sad thoughts, for we believed that within a few days we too would be employed in exactly the same way. We were informed that we would disembark on the 29th.

On the 27th we received a visit from the catholic Bishop and a priest.[9] These reverend gentlemen had learnt that a particular vessel coming from Canada had on board a certain number of French-Canadian prisoners, all Catholics,[10] and thinking that their visit would be agreeable to us, they came to see us. The bishop was an Englishmen, and his secretary an Irishman; both spoke French. They asked us several questions and inquired into the state of our health, details of our voyage, etc; we conversed for about an hour and a half, we speaking always with the greatest respect. They told us that they would see that no obstacle would be placed in the way of ourcarrying out our religious duties, and they terminated their kindly visit by a prayer that they said amongst us. The bishop gave us his blessing, at the same time saying that he would return on the following day. This unexpected visit caused us a great deal of pleasure and afforded us some little consolation.[11]

On the 28th the Bishop came back to see us, with his secretary and another priest. We were agreeably surprised at the interest taken by these reverend gentlemen in our misfortune, and to see that they did not worry about the difficulty and danger of climbing up and down the ship's side again on ladders, and of seeking us out on the lower deck, a dark and uncomfortable place, so as to extend to us their sympathy. Mr Brady – this was the secretary's name – prayed, and asked whether anyone wished to make a confession. We said we all did. They then confessed some of us, but having business which called them elsewhere, they went away, telling us that they would return the next day, hear the confessions of the remainder, and administer the sacrament to those who were so disposed; we had only to prepare a place suitable for saying Mass. They told us also that the Governor, Sir George Gipp(s), this very day was trying to make up his mind whether he would allow us to disembark at Sydney or assign us to some other place. Having come such a great distance, and being so tired after so long a voyage, we were very dejected when we heard this news.

On the 29th at eight o'clock in the morning, Monsignor and his Secretary, in accordance with their promise, came and heard the confessions of those whom they had not been able to hear the evening before; and at ten o'clock Monsignor said, in the depths of the hold where we were lodged, a low mass, upon an altar built of our boxes by those amongst us who were best qualified to do such work; a number of images that we had added to some articles brought by these reverend gentlemen made the altar quite seemly. Doubtless God found it so, for it was a work of the most ardent devotion. At the end of the Mass, Monsignor offered up some long prayers; and his secretary brought this simple and very touching ceremony to an end by an appropriate sermon. We were all most gratified and affected to see these respectable gentlemen extend their zeal for religion and their charity so far, and particularly to see the Bishop come and crawl about for three days in succession in the depths of a ship's hold, so as to bring us back to Jesus Christ, and to console us in our tribulations.

On the 1st of March, as a result of the news that we had heard, namely, that His Excellency was still undecided whether he would cause us to be disembarked at Sydney or hasten our transfer to another colony, we drew up an address to Mr Brady, signed by all of us, so that he might beg Monsignor to intercede for us with his Excellency, and make plain to him the desire we had of passing the time of our exile in this colony; that the fatigues of a long voyage, added to those of a long imprisonment at Montreal, had greatly distressed us: that many of us were old and sick, and that our dearest wish was to settle down in this place. This address was placed in the hands of the surgeon of the ship, who sent it on to its proper destination. This same day we received a visit from several gentlemen, who found that we had very good manners, and that we all had fine features, qualities apparently somewhat remarkable amongst rebels.

From the 2nd to the 3rd we gained no positive information about our fate, only that the question of deciding whether we should be located in Sydney or be removed farther away had caused much difference of opinion in the Council. We knew well that the country was rich and that fruits grew there in abundance.

Nothing remarkable occurred on the 4th. The weather was very hot. The deck of the vessel scorched our feet. The gnats or mosquitoes worried us greatly. They penetrated even into the between-decks where we lay.

On the 5th a sergeant came to warn us that we were to be reviewed at two o'clock in the afternoon, and, consequently, that we were to make ourselves ready. In due course, at about three o 'clock, three persons came on board, and immediatelv we were called up on deck, and in succession were pointed out and named. We were asked our age, birth place, occupation, whether we were married or single, whether we could read and write, etc.[12]

At ten a.m. on the 6th we were ordered up on deck, and were examined from head to foot. The most detailed description of each of us was recorded. Our features, the colour of our hair and of our eyes, the number of teeth missing, all the marks that we had on our bodies, hands and legs - nothing was omitted. We still did not know where we were to be disembarked.

On the 7th we received the reply to the address we had made to Mr. Brady to be transmitted to the Bishop. Here is a copy of it:-

Windsor, 6th March 1840.

Gentlemen and well-beloved in our Saviour Jesus Christ,

I hasten to reply to your letter; I fear that it arrived a little late. I have just received it at 6 o'clock to-day; I am about to send it on to Monsignor, praying him to exercise his influence with the Governor so that he may take into consideration your unfortunate position. I pray always that the Lord will give you patience, courage, and a place of rest after your long and painful voyage, and especially a location where it will he easy for you to carry out the duties of your holy religion; and may the grace of our Lord be with all of you.

Believe me for life,

Your very affectionate servant,
(Signed) L' ABBE BRADY, Missionary.

So the 8th and 9th passed by without our learning anything in connexion with our disembarkation. We were in complete ignorance concerning what was to be done with us; it was a subject of conjecture amongst us all.

On the 10th at four o'clock in the evening, a sergeant came and warned us to prepare to disembark the following day. This news caused us much joy. The long drawn-out anxiety with which we had been tormented concerning our fate was at last dispelled.

On the 11th, after we had folded up our beds which were to serve us in the settlement to which we were going, we were sent with our chests and bags on board a large boat and transported eight miles from Sydney to a penal settlement called Longbottom.[13] At about eleven o'clock in the morning we landed there. Some soldiers who were in charge of this settlement came to receive us, and led us a distance of about a mile from the beach where we first arrived to a kind of barracks or gaol built in the form of a square. There were also several little detached buildings, such, e.g., as a cookhouse, a shed, etc. Very soon after our arrival, a sergeant, who was in command of the platoon of soldiers who were stationed there, as well as of those who had brought us, had us all lined up, and began in a most uncouth way to set out the boundaries of this settlement, as well as the regulations which we had to observe. He told us that if we broke the prescribed bounds we would be liable to fifty lashes, and that we were forbidden, under penalty of severe punishment, to wander about the interior of the settlement without permission, and that for neglect of our set tasks we would also be punished with the lash; for disobedience or lack of respect to our superior; and for various other infractions of little consequence we would be rigorously punished. If the reader will keep for a moment his attention fixed on the terms of this harangue, and if he considers especially the arrogant vehemence with which it was uttered, he will get some idea of the prospect which our future offered us. About five o 'clock in the evening we were called together, and, after having been checked, we were placed in certain of the prison quarters and shut up there under lock and key until the following day. We were compelled to lie down early, and on our beds which were provided with nothing but a single blanket. Strict silence had to be observed during the evening, as well as the whole night long. At six o'clock in the morning the doors were opened, and we went out to get our breakfast. It consisted of a thick soup made from half a pound of maize or Indian corn flour and an ounce of sugar. At noon we had a pound of bread made from the most inferior quality of flour, and a pound of meat, either beef or mutton, and nothing more, except for the carters, the mechanics and the foreman, who received a slight addition of tea and sugar. Never did we have anything for supper. After having laboured the whole day, worn out with hunger and fatigue, about half past five or six o'clock in the evening we were locked up.

The second day after our arrival, we obtained permission to wash out the room where we had to sleep. Until our arrival it had been occupied by several hundred prisoners who had been sent elsewhere to make room for us. But, unfortunately for us, they had not carried away with them all their filth and their vermin; and their quarters, now become ours, were disgustingly dirty. During the course of the same day, we were all assembled and informed that the clothes that we were wearing were going to be branded, and that we would be permitted to wear these same clothes until the first of May, the day on which the Government would distribute clothes to the prisoners, clothes which consist of a waistcoat and pair of trousers made of heavy grey cloth, a cotton shirt, a pair of shoes and a grey cap, all branded in heavy letters; this outfit is to last for six months, and is the winter issue. In November we receive another issue of lighter summer clothing, for it is in this month that the great heat waves of the year begin. We were compelled to submit ourselves to this very humiliating business; and all our boxes and bags with their contents were put away in the Government stores to be returned to us when we obtained our freedom. On the third day we were sent out to hard labour. Some of us broke stones, others carted them on to the roads with bullocks harnessed to carts; one party of us was finally employed repairing the public highways. Each gang of men was in the custody of a soldier. This military superintendence lasted for about a month, a space of time during which we worked very hard, being badly nourished, badly bedded, locked up every night, and deprived of every means of communication whatsoever.

At the end of a month or thereabouts, a change in our settlement took place. The Governor withdrew the soldiers who kept watch over us, and replaced them by a single person charged with the care of us. This particular person chose from amongst us those whom he thought most suitable to fill the office of overseers in charge of our fellow-countrymen, and assigned to each his respective task; thus we were under the superintendence of our own selves, though it was still difficult for us to take things easy; for, every day there came inspectors to examine our work, and they were well prepared to criticize, if they came to the conclusion that we had not toiled hard enough. They were able to submit reports against us, from which later on we would have suffered the consequences, so that it was necessary for us to be diligent with our work during the whole of the time that we were held to forced labour.

I had the advantage of becoming one of the overseers, and I had the good fortune to be able to procure, as far as circumstances permitted, some amelioration of the hard conditions of those prisoners whose control was entrusted to me; and all those who shared duties similar to mine did as much for their charges. Whatever material advantage we obtained, however, came as a result of the following circumstance. It arose from the fact that we were alone at this settlement, and especially because our superintendent, who had always been a lieutenant in the army, was not, to tell the truth, a very good judge of work; so we could sometimes induce him to accept anything offered. Do not believe, however, that this benefit was the result of his good nature or his humanity; it was derived from his ignorance. For it must be said he was a veritable tyrant, a man without character, one given to abusing his power, in order to ill-treat us every time he could find an opportunity of doing so. He never came to see us except for the pleasure of picking a quarrel: and that is the sum total of the matter; we can assert, too, that if we were not punished, it was entirely due to our good behaviour, to our patience, and to bur constancy in manfully enduring much ill-treatment that we suffered daily, and not to the humanity of our despotic superintendent whose name was Henry Clinton Badly *(sic.)*.[14] Nevertheless, several of us, in spite of all the precautions taken against arousing his animosity, were punished with the dark cells, and daily tormented and ill-used in the most painful and disgusting way, without his having regard for the age of the person who was often insulted by unseemly threats. This man, so aptly named Baddly *(sic.)*, had been clothed with unlimited power over us by the Governor. In vain we voiced our complaints; they were not heard. We also made an application for an increase in our rations, explaining that it was impossible for us to stand up to work as hard as ours without an improvement in our wretched food, etc. The reply of the authorities was that it was the ration allowed to prisoners, and that we had to be satisfied with it; in a word, that we were held to be in the same category as the most criminal of the convicts, performing exactly the same tasks, wearing exactly the same costume, and subject to the same punishments.

After eight or nine months of a miserable existence such as this, His Excellency Sir George Gipps decided to make some enquiries about us. By a lucky chance, our superintendent was well inclined towards us and submitted a favourable report. We made use of the opportunity to beg him to ask his Excellency's permission to delay a little the hour of our confinement after the day's toil. We were granted an additional hour. A little while after this happening, our superintendent conceived the idea of turning our services to his own profit rather than to that of the Government; consequently he employed us much more frequently working for himself to the prejudice of the Government, and obtained the whole of the fruit of our labours. But as can readily be imagined, we did not lose by it, we had to keep silence concerning this fraud on account of the little privileges we thereby obtained. As for ourselves, it mattered little to us whether we were working for the Government or for anybody else, being, as we were, responsible only for obedience to the superintendent, and being able to obtain any amelioration to our situation only by sharing his interests and flattering his wishes. Nothing is more natural than that a prisoner should seek to improve his lot, especially when the Government alone is the sufferer. In recompense, therefore, for the work done for our superintendent, and for our discreet behaviour, he extended for still another hour the time of our freedom from confinement. In addition, he allowed us to employ for our own profit the hours apart from our ordinary labours. We occupied ourselves then, gathering shells along the shores of the Bay which surrounded us; these we afterwards sold to the boatmen who conveyed them to Sydney or to Parramatta, where they sold them again to be made into lime. In this country this is the sole source from which this necessary substance can be obtained, for there is no limestone here. All this was work done at night, for secrecy was essential for us. What we made by this trading, added to the profit from the selling of wood, that, following the example of the superintendent, we carried on, provided us with sufficient money to procure those articles of which we felt the greatest need; in his turn, our superintendent was compelled to keep his eyes shut about these happenings. Sometime later he fell ill, and was compelled to keep to his bed. Nevertheless, this misfortune did not prevent him from carrying on his trade, and consequently us from continuing ours, without, however, neglecting our daily work During this period, I was appointed, with two of my compatriots, to act as night-watchman at the settlement, a custom which prevailed all the time we were there, and which exists in all penal establishments as much to provide for the safety of the settlement as to keep a watch so that no prisoner may escape. As far as we were concerned, there was nothing to fear in this connexion, but an established rule had to be observed. In the same way, taking advantage of the illness of our superintendent, we closed the gates at the usual hour; but as soon as our superior officer had retired to give himself over to the suffering which overcame him, we opened the gates again, and went out to carry on our own private work. Occasionally there was a certain amount of confusion. But, on the stroke of one o'clock, very early in the morning, we all returned in correct order, and to our proper places, and no one could have said that anything irregular had taken place. Thus, every night we were at liberty, every day in subjection. During our stay at this settlement we had the grief to see die, in the hospital, two of our companions, Louis Doumouchel,[15] who died of dropsy, and Gabriel Chevrefils, who succumbed probably to the same disease. During our residence at this place we went several times to mass at Parramatta, a little town seven miles distant from our location, and often Catholic priests came and said mass in our midst, in an oratory that we had prepared for this purpose, the best that circumstances would permit us.[16] Such was the state of affairs when we learned that the Governor had decided to assign all of us to various employers for the space of six months at the rate of thirty shillings per month for those who had no trade, and forty for those who had one. One half of our wages was to be placed in the Savings Bank, to be returned to us when we were set at liberty; and the other half to be paid to us every week, with the understanding that our employer was compelled to provide us with board and lodging. Accordingly each of us was assigned, and we found ourselves widely separated after about two years' forced labour for the Government. For myself, I was to reside in Sydney at the residence of a furniture maker in the capacity of clerk, salesman and collector. During this period, Bishop Polding, the Catholic Bishop of Sydney, left for Europe. We had provided him with a petition to present to His Majesty, requesting certain improvements in our condition. He had the kindness to offer to present it himself to the Colonial Secretary, and to undertake to do all in his power to bring it to a successful issue. The result was that five months after we had been assigned, we learned that a Ticket-of-Leave, that is, a permission to work on our own account or otherwise as we wished in anyone of the Districts of the Colony that we were pleased to select, had been granted us. Those who had settled down in the Sydney District were instructed to present themselves at the Police Station on the second day of each month to answer to their names, and those from the other districts on the first of January. The slightest infraction of the penal laws was to entail the loss of these privileges and our return to Government service. Thus we remained until the date of our pardon. This interval was very painful for all of us, for, in addition to the fact that we were isolated from one another, we were compelled to work very hard and for small wages. A certain number of us were constrained to accept occupations to which they were utter strangers, and outside their own branch of industry.

When the Government decided to assign us to particular individuals in the colony, each of those who wished to have us in their service had to come and seek us out at the establishment where we were working, and it is my duty and a justice I owe to my companions to mention here the following facts, so as to make known how we were treated in this respect. As we all were considered of good character, and it was acknowledged throughout the whole country that we were honest and useful persons, each employer hastened to put in an application for our services. As is customary, those occupying the highest positions in the Government had the preference, and the Chief Superintendent of Convicts, whose name was Captain MacLean, [17] came seeking some ten of us. Another man, Sir Thomas Mitchell, Surveyor-General and member of the Council, obtained three or four; the Deputy Surveyor-General, named Mr Perry,[18] had five or six; Mr Dumas,[19] chief clerk of the Government departments, had five or six, of which number I was one. All those particular gentlemen had the benefit of our services for more than eighteen months after the two years of our servitude for the Government had expired, but giving us only a small part of the wages that they had agreed to pay us. Seeing that we could not obtain any satisfaction from them, we asked for our discharge and the total amount of our salary, so that we might reside elsewhere. They gave us our discharge willingly enough, but, as for our wages, they told us to come back again later and they would pay us. Who would have believed that we would have been the dupes of these great men! In due course, at the end of a specified time we returned to our respective gentlemen to request the performance of their promises. Again we were told to return later. Finally, they ended up by threatening us, and told us never to return again or worry them in the future, for they would find means of ending that degree of liberty which we had, and would have us returned to Government work. Some of us carried our complaints concerning the conduct of these officers to the Governor. All the answer we got was to be told that we could recover at law. But how, in our poverty, could we wrestle legally with rich and influential men - men who, in the issue, would have found all sorts of opportunities of injuring us. When we received news of our pardon we made one last attempt to get satisfaction from these thieves. On this occasion they could not tell us that they could have us punished, for we were free men like themselves; but they told us that it was impossible for them to pay us at this time, since they were without ready cash. Vainly did we represent to them that, without money, a great number of us would not be able to see again our native land and our families; that consequently we were deprived of that which was dearest to us in the world, the happiness for which we had so much longed. All this had not the slightest effect on these men, whose souls held no pity. Their greed had suggested to them that we would not wait until the next law term, and that no sacrifice would make us refuse the first opportunity of leaving these shores. Thus they would be able to rob us of more than three hundred pounds-sterling which was due to us in a lump sum; that is, more than was necessary to restore to their native hearths our fifteen unfortunate poor companions who, through lack of means, were now compelled to see the rest of us embark for Canada, the country that as one company we had so much set our hearts upon. Thus, instead of being protected as we hoped by these high officials, we were merely their dupes. What should anyone now think of the lower classes, when the highest of all were the first to cheat you!

At last, in April, 1844, we learned that five of our compatriots had received their pardons. This news caused much joy to the recipients, but much pain to the others, for the latter believed that His Majesty's clemency was limited to the granting of pardons to these five alone. Some, however, were of opinion that pardons had been granted to all, but that we would receive the news only by groups and at different periods. It was a subject of lively conjecture for all of us. One unexpected circumstance stabilized our ideas. In the interval of waiting, I received from Canada a letter which informed me as a certainty of the approaching pardon of all the prisoners in New South Wales, because at that very time active steps in our favour were being taken in Canada, and that there was every prospect of success. The date of this letter convinced us that there they were unaware of the pardoning of the five of us, a matter concerning which I have spoken a little previously. Moreover, on the very day that I received my letter we heard that the pardon of twenty other Canadians had been granted; I was not, however, amongst this number. Nevertheless, neither myself nor the others any longer doubted that the same favour would very shortly be extended to the remainder - that it was no longer a matter for jocularity, but a serious question. At last, on the 24th June, I was informed that my pardon as well as those of all the other Canadians had arrived. So, from this day, with several others I began to concentrate on my departure, and to endeavour to find as quickly as possible a passage from a land so full of horror for all of us.

New South Wales has its good points just as all other countries have. Its air is very healthy and its climate temperate and pleasant. In this country set in the middle of the ocean, and within the tropics, the sun in summer, it is true, is burning hot; but the sea breeze springs up round about ten o 'clock in the morning and refreshes the whole countryside. Winter is the season of the year the most pleasant ill the world; rarely does it freeze there, and only in the interior and on the highlands is there any hoar frost; there, a little snow occasionally falls.

Sometimes winter manifests itself by heavy falls of rain, accompanied by violent winds which often last for whole months. Then the roads are in such a bad state that great inconvenience results, especially for travellers and for carriers of produce from the interior to Sydney and other shipping places; the products consist of wool, tallow, grain, etc. In the interior the soil is very fertile; all the various grains and vegetables of the finest quality grow in abundance; all the European fruits, such as oranges, lemons, peaches, pears, apples, etc., flourish there in profusion, and consequently are sold cheaply. The soil is also very suitable for the vine, which produces plenty of excellent grapes. Unfortunately, however, it is only of late that attention has been given to its cultivation which should have been and in future will be one of the greatest resources of the country. In this connexion the English settlers are much indebted for the introduction of so useful a commodity to certain Frenchmen[20] who some years ago came and settled in this country, and having promoted in the inhabitants a taste for the culture of the vine, have taught them the method of cultivating it, and then of extracting from it a wine which today is preferred to the wines which come from abroad. There can now be seen in New South Wales young vineyards of thirty, forty, fifty and sixty acres in area. The culture and the care of these are always entrusted to Frenchmen, who are highly expert in this branch. As for the English, they know nothing at all about it.

The grain harvest is not regularly as abundant as that of the vegetables and fruits, for the drought sometimes causes great destruction. There have been years when there was no rain for nine or the months. Then all the grain and even the grass are burnt up before they reach maturity; the streams, the wells, the tanks, the springs, all are dried up ; and thousands of persons may be seen going miles to seek for water for their own personal use. In other years exactly the opposite happens. The rains are so abundant and continuous that the whole country is flooded for some weeks; consequently all the crops perish and many other serious results ensue. For example, houses and stables are overturned, bridges and fences broken down, cattle destroyed, etc.; many persons lose their lives, all communications being cut off by the great body of water. The result is that, being subject either to one or other of these two calamities, the harvest is never assured. The country is rather a pastoral than an agricultural one. Nature seems to have designed it particularly for the former. No country possesses so much rich pasturage; the fields are covered from one of the year to the other with grass, abundant and evergreen. There can also be seen immense numbers of cattle, horses and sheep. Therein lies the great source of the wealth of the country, and that from which is derived the principal branch of commerce. The cattle hardly ever suffer from the capriciousness of the climate; the cold spells are not severe enough to be taken much notice of. The shade of the great forests protects them from the fierce heat of the sun. The rains are to them the most distressing element: but since these are in general only transitory, the animals are so accustomed to them that they suffer no ill effects as a result. When these details are kept in mind, it ought not to appear improbable to see individual landowners possessing from five to six thousand horses, from fifteen to twenty thousand cattle, eighty to a hundred thousand sheep, some more, some fewer, of which the innumerable flocks are scattered in different districts throughout the immense spaces of the colony. After the sheep-shearing is over, for more than two months great loads of wool can be seen corning in, done up in bales and ready to be placed on board ship; for it is the principal article of export, together with salt beef, skins, tallow and several other articles. The export of these articles has been greatly increased as a result of the great depression in all colonial affairs since 1842, a period during which the prices of cattle and of all colonial products have suffered a very great depreciation. The owners of these immense flocks and herds no longer being able to hold in reserve sufficient of their profits even to pay the wages of the large number of employés that the care of their cattle necessitated; the revenue of their immense farms being no longer sufficient to pay for the actual work done, still much less to support the luxury in which these rich farmers live, they have consequently been compelled to boil down the cattle for the sake of the tallow and the skins that they export to England, as well as to reduce the number of their flocks and their domestic servants, and in this way to cut down their expenses. Besides this, we see cattle and sheep in thousands being brought down to Sydney to be slaughtered there or in some neighbouring locality convenient for shipping abroad, so as to avoid the expenses of transport.

This great change in the commercial affairs of the colony is due in part to the large number of emigrants who have been arriving in droves since 1841, all poor people, bringing not a penny into the country, and, as can be imagined, having to share with the others whatever they possessed, a condition of affairs which brought about a reduction in the wages of every class of workman, a scarcity of money, and in the end the decline of the colony. Hitherto, the farmers and others had had the advantage of having in their service as many convicts as they desired, having only to maintain them and paying them no wages whatsoever. This was the system under which the colony was established, and thus were made the fortunes of so many citizens of

New South Wales; that is to say, at the expense of the sweat and toil of these unfortunates, who cleared their lands for them without its costing them a single penny.

But in 1841 the deportation of convicts from Great Britain and her colonies to Sydney ceased, so that they could not, as previously, have the workmen without paying for them. They were compelled to pay for the carrying out of their work, and, the produce of the land falling to a very low price, they were not able to support the condition of luxury in which they lived. Consequently they found themselves for the most part bankrupt within the space of two years. The country then received its emancipation and was given a constitution; but, at the time of our departure, this act of goodwill had not brought about any change in the shocking condition of a host of emigrants and others of the working class, who blocked up the highroads and the streets, crying aloud their woes through lack of employment. Those who were in work complained also about the reduction in their, wages; thus there was an outcry of universal misery from one end of the colony to the other. Affairs were in this critical condition when we took our departure.

REPORT

In New South Wales there is a large number of aborigines. The Europeans have never been able to bring them to any degree of civilization. They are the most stupid and most disgusting race of men in the world. They are divided into tribes which are ever on the move; they never sleep twice in the same place, and always in the open air without any shelter. They live on kangaroos, opossums, goannas, snakes and other animals that they catch and eat raw. They do not wear any kind of clothing. They are dirty and extremely fierce. Nevertheless, the tribes in the vicinity of Sydney and of other places inhabited by Europeans have lost a little of their savageness and of their natural bad habits. (They are all cannibals.) But, it has never been possible to persuade them to work or to improve their condition. These degraded and useless beings can be seen prowling round the towns in gangs, begging alms. They have scarcely a stitch of clothes on them, for the most strenuous efforts of the Europeans have not succeeded in keeping clothes on them. Each tribe has its king whose distinctive mark is a little copper plate in the shape of a half-moon, which hangs round his neck, and on which is written the name of his tribe. This mark of distinction is given them by the colonists. Formerly they had a mark made by themselves, one somewhat of the same shape as that of today, these kings are often to be seen at the head of a party of their subjects going hunting. They never like to sleep under a roof, preferring the open air to a shelter. They are extremely ugly, fairly tall, but thin and active. The tribes of the interior are all wild. Sometimes they rush upon the European settlements, massacre all those who resist their attacks, pillage and carry off herds of cattle and flocks of sheep, and drive them into the mountains or other places known only to themselves, where they satisfy their voracious appetites. These disastrous attacks have compelled several settlers to abandon their farms and to return closer to Sydney, so as to secure themselves and their belongings from the rapacity of these formidable brigands. The slightest excuse is sufficient cause for a conflict between them; one tribe, for example, carries off a blanket, a knife or some similar object, and immediately you see the offended tribe up in arms against the other. Their weapons consist of a long spear that they throw with remarkable dexterity. They rarely miss an object that they catch sight of within a distance of thirty paces. I have seen one of them throw a spear into the key-hole of a lock placed twenty-five paces from him, and repeat this feat several times without missing.

The incident that I am about to relate is a very striking proof of the preference that these savages have for their own barbarous and miserable life as contrasted with one civilized and pleasant; and of the supreme disgust that they have naturally for every touch of civilization.

When Governor Phillip was recalled to England, he took away with him one of these natives whom he called Benelong.[21] For two years he kept him in England, living in great comfort. He made particularly strong efforts to turn him away from his barbaric habits, and to inspire in him as many as possible of the principles of civilization, so that he could derive from them some advantages when he returned amongst his fellow countrymen. The savage seemed well able to understand the Governor's intention, and promised to co-operate. However, after two years, the Governor sent him back to the country of his birth to rejoin his fellows, believing he had made an important contribution to the welfare of the colony. But, to the great surprise of all, he was no sooner ashore on his native land than he stripped himself of all his good clothes, cast them aside, and, rushing into the depths of the bush, went off to rejoin his beloved tribe, from which he never again returned. He was seen again wandering about just as wild as his brothers, and following all his native inclinations.

The indigenous animals of the country are the kangaroo, the opossum, the native dog, and several small quadrupeds of little importance: the most remarkable is the kangaroo, which is as large as the largest greyhound, but while being quite as fine in the forequarters as the latter, they are much bigger in the rest of the body; their head is narrow, the hind legs from five to six feet long, but the forelegs ten or twelve inches only, and the tail at least four feet long and thick as the lower part of a man's leg. They neither walk nor run; they move forward only by leaps, helping themselves by their hind paws and their tail, so as to give themselves a spring, and use their fore paws to enable them to stop. When they are pursued they make leaps of from fifteen to eighteen feet, and move so quickly that greyhounds, even those best trained for hunting, have difficulty in catching them. Often they break with their tails the paws of the dogs that are hunting them – so powerful are they – by means of this sole weapon of defence which Nature has given them; people have often seen – and other persons well worthy of credence have assured me of the truth of the matter – kangaroos, surprised by a single man, grab hold of him by their fore paws and carry him to the nearest swamp, or to the edge of a precipice, and immediately would have killed him there, had it not been for the arrival of some rescuers; many, deprived of this timely assistance, have suffered death from these animals. I have been told that there are many much larger than those of which I have just spoken, and that they are extraordinarily powerful. The largest that I saw were five feet long (the tail of course, not included). The flesh is of delicious taste; the skin makes excellent leather. It takes the place of calf-skin, to which it is much superior, as much on account of its suppleness, which, without splitting, resists the heat of the climate, as of the fineness and beauty of its texture.

The opossum is the size of our wild cats, like which it also lives in hollow trees, to the branches of which they often hang by the tail. The females, like those of the kangaroo, carry a pouch beneath their stomach, in which their young take refuge in case of danger, and where they also find the milk which nourishes them. The dogs called "native", in size and in colour much resemble our foxes. They often make cruel attacks on sheep and poultry. There are flying squirrels of various kinds. There exist various species of venomous snakes. The most remarkable are those called black snakes. They are from four to twenty feet long, and very venomous. The diamond snake is even more so. He has the unpleasant habit of climbing trees, stretching himself out along the branches, and then dropping on to his prey. There is an infinite number of birds of wonderful plumage; but none resemble our Canadian birds, except the crows, which differ from ours only in the quality of their cawing. The most striking of the birds in this country is the celebrated Bird of Paradise, which is too well known to need describing here. There is also the Emu, a kind of ostrich, five or six feet high, whose body is as big as that of a sheep. It has a long neck and a small head. Their wings are not in proportion to their weight, and serve only to increase the speed of their running, which this quality as well as their long claws make very swift; so much so, indeed, that a horse at full gallop would have difficulty in catching up with them. In addition, there are to be seen numerous flocks of parakeets of all sizes and colours. We kill them simply with the blow of a stick. There are to be found wood-pigeons very similar to ours, and black swans, but very few ducks.

But there are other living beings much more terrible than those I have mentioned. One scourge (the term is most appropriate) which ravages the country, and which is the absolute terror of travellers as well as of all the inhabitants generally, is what they call in English the Bushrangers, that is to say escapees who have taken to the bush. These escapees form a class of men wholly depraved, and stripped of every shred of morality; men absolutely incorrigible, steeped in crime, who have escaped from the penal settlements and the masters to whom they were assigned, and have taken refuge in the woods, there to live by robbing and brigandage. Some of them live in bands and under a leader, who seldom fails to be the boldest of them all. Hardly any travellers can escape the watchful rapacity of these bandits, who hold them up and rob them of all their possessions. And, if they offer the least resistance, they are often killed on the spot, and always wounded, for these robbers are always armed.

Often, at night, they attack the homes of peaceful citizens, rob them and carry off all they can carry, stopping at nothing, even murder, to overcome any resistance. Although concerning them the laws are very severe, and the police very powerful, nevertheless the woods are infested with these robbers: it is absolutely dangerous to travel into the interior of the country and even to reside there. Moreover, one is never safe, even in the streets of the town. Sometimes a man will come and meet you, or will catch up with you on the road, and, without showing any apparent intention towards you, will even enter into a conversation with you. Then, if he finds a favourable opportunity, will attack you at the very moment when you are least thinking about it, either with a cudgel or a knife that he has in his hand, will lie you low, will rob you of what you have on you, and run away. Such an occurrence has happened very often in the town. Every day, and often several times a day, these shocking scenes are repeated. Sydney is the haunt of the greater part of these highwaymen, who have the audacity to disguise themselves and walk about the streets publicly in the midst of policemen and other citizens. It has been several times revealed that these wretches from outback used to keep up corre-spondence with their fellows in Sydney, that the former used to send their stolen property from the country so that the latter could dispose of it and send them back the money in return.

I have now only to set forth what happens to them when they are captured; for the laws have no consideration for them, and their least punishment is imprisonment for life in irons. Ought one to be surprised at such occurrences in a country where the total population is from a hundred and sixty to a hundred and eighty thousand souls, of whom sixty thousand are made up of the vilest, the most demoralized and the most wicked in Great Britain and her colonies.[22] That is to say, of the forty thousand men and forty thousand women who constitute the original colonization of this country,[23] the greater part, far from reforming themselves, have become more and more inured to crime, and have constantly gone further and further in their acts of lawlessness. The small number of those who have endeavoured to behave themselves well forms today the richest section of the colony. Sydney contains a population of thirty thousand people; it is built upon Port Jackson, nine miles from its entrance.

The port is one of the most beautiful and one of the safest that it would be possible to discover. Ships lying there need have no fears.

RETURN FROM SYDNEY TO ENGLAND

On the 9th July, 1844, we embarked, to the number of 38,[24] on board the ship *Achilles,* Captain Heale, our destination being London. The remainder of our brothers in exile, not being able to pay their passage money, were compelled to stay behind. On the morning of the 10th we raised our anchor, and, favoured by a light breeze, reached the mouth of the harbour, where we cast anchor to await the customs-house examination which usually takes place when a ship is going out to sea. We were lined up for inspection and identification; then, about four o'clock p.m., we raised anchor again, and about seven a 'clock departed, leaving behind us, to our great regret, fifteen[25] of our compatriots. It was with heartful satisfaction that we said farewell to New South Wales, which had been to us a prison for more than four years.

On the 11th we had a very strong north-westerly wind, which blew us along in a very favourable direction, for we were beading for Cape Horn. In the evening we saw four or five whales. During the night, the wind changed to a violent westerly, so that we made nine knots an hour on the right course. It is useless to express the delight we all felt at removing so rapidly from this land, which had been for us so long a place of pain and suffering, while every moment we were drawing closer to our homeland, our families and our friends.

On the 12th the same wind continued to blow with the same force. We were compelled to lower the topsails; several of us were seasick, but much less so than on the first voyage, which must be attributed to the superior quality of the food, as well as to the freedom to walk about on deck from morning to evening, and from evening to morning. About six o'clock the wind increased to such a degree that several of us became terrified, and during the night the ship was so tossed about that we could scarcely remain in our beds. Each wave brought on board a great volume of water, the wind being accompanied by a thunderstorm.

On the 13th the same wind, but much more violent, now and again a thunderstorm, the heavens clouded over, the sea extremely heavy, at every moment the deck submerged by the waves. We made our way ever in a favourable direction towards Cape Horn. We soon began to notice that the weather was growing colder as we advanced to the South, for our course was South-East.

On the 14th the wind was still from the same direction, but less violent. We had several thunderstorms during the course of the day.

On the 15th the wind was very fierce, west-south-west, accompanied by storms; the sea was so heavy that we were compelled to go below to the between-decks for protection against the waves which swamped the main deck. The number of sick decreased; we continued to make good progress.

16th: The same wind, but a little more moderate than yesterday; several storms during the course of the day; strong wind during the night.

17th: Calm weather the whole day.

18th: Very strong north-west wind, accompanied by rain; the sea very much disturbed; water swamped the ship during the whole day; several of us are very frightened; as evening approached, the bad weather increased still more, but died down during the night.

19th: Fine weather, fresh and favourable wind; we passed to the north of New Zealand, and made good progress towards Cape Horn.

20th: Wind N.W., stronger than yesterday, accompanied by rain and thunder. At 4 o'clock p.m., a heavy storm. The night was one of the roughest that we had to suffer since the date of our departure. We could not sleep on account of the rolling of the vessel. The sea washes continually over the deck, so that it terrifies some of us.

On the 21st the wind blew with the same violence; the sea is very heavy, the ship is extraordinarily shaken; nevertheless we suffer these inconveniences with courage, and that so much the more so because the tempest carries us in the right direction.

22nd: Moderate wind, with a thunderstorm; we go forward speedily.

23rd: Weather calm and fine. We caught two albatrosses on a fishing line. It is very curious that birds with wings so great cannot fly when they are on a flat solid surface. We threw them on the deck, and they walked from one end of it to the other without even trying to take flight. They are excellent eating.

The 24th, 25th, 26th and 27th were one long succession of bad weather; the wind, an extraordinarily strong southerly accompanied by rain and sometimes hail. The waves never ceased to cover completely the deck of the ship; in addition, the rolling of the vessel was terrible; the sea is in a fury; the waves rise to a terrifying height.

The 28th was a subject for argument. According to our method of counting the days since our departure, we were convinced that it was Sunday. The Captain himself maintained that this day should be regarded as Saturday. It is not necessary to say that he got his way. The weather was calm the whole day and enabled us to recover our strength. Our health had suffered much from the bad weather during these last few days; the wind freshened towards evening.

On the 29th terrible weather; the wind contrary and of terrifying force; it was accompanied by rain, hail and cold. We were compelled to set the vessel's course for "The Cape," as the English say; that is, to place her in the position most suitable for restricting the hurricane. Only those persons who have any knowledge of navigation can have an exact idea of the state of a vessel bound for the Cape in a raging sea. It was a veritable tempest. The vessel rose to a terrible height, and fell as it were into an abyss. One would have said that the ship was about to be swallowed up every instant. It was impossible for us to remain on deck.

30th: Though the wind has moderated a little it is still contrary. We are making between seven and eight miles an hour; the weather is clear.

1st of August: The wind S.W., a little contrary to our set course; the weather dull and stormy, with fog; the weather is always very bad at this particular season of the year. The fine season extends from December to February.

2nd: Wind fresh and favourable. The sea has quite calmed down, the weather fine. We caught some birds which are called Cape Penguins, about the same size as our pigeons. They are very good to eat.

3rd: Weather fine and almost calm. It is the first day; I believe, since our departure, that it has not rained.

4th, 5th and 6th: A fair wind, but weather overcast and accompanied by rain and hail. We continued to make excellent progress during these three days at the rate of six or seven miles an hour.

7th, 8th and 9th: A strong westerly wind accompanied by rain and hail. We continue to advance directly for Cape Horn; it hailed during these last three nights.

10th: Still the same wind as on the previous evening; the sky is overcast, heavy cloud portending a tempest. Several fogs which occurred during the day brought back to us memories of the climate of Canada. About nine o'clock in the evening, the storm which had been threatening all day broke with tremendous fury. The waves rose to a terrifying height; the ship climbed as it were to the top of lofty mountains, and then fell with all her weight into a deep gulf. The water rushed in vast quantities over the ship; the wind blew furiously, with hail, rain and lightning, so that it might be said that all the elements were in league to destroy us. Our ship was as knocked about as though it had been exposed to the fire of a battle; the sails were torn to ribbons, the shrouds broken, the boards which served as a protection round the ship were smashed and carried overboard. Some barrels which were fastened in the deck broke adrift; they were thrown into the sea by the sailors to prevent accidents. The ship creaked and shook with the shocks of the sea: two men were tied to the steering-wheel. All this happened during the darkest of nights.

On the 11th, the bad weather continued with the same violence. The deck revealed the most terrifying scene. Everything there was smashed and ruined; water covered it knee-deep; it was impossible to remain there. The sailors had never seen a storm so frightful nor one of so long duration. During these last two days we sailed between two lanes of water as dark as though it were night.

On the 12th, 13th and 14th the wind moderated a little, although it still blew very violently from the west; the weather was overcast, stormy and very cold; there was a fall of snow. To our satisfaction, we are rapidly approaching Cape Horn.

On the 15th the wind had almost entirely dropped; but the sea was rough, the weather very cold; the sun shone for the first time for a fortnight.

16th: Sky overcast, strong wind from the west, the sea was extremely disturbed; appearance of bad weather towards evening. The night passed peacefully enough.

17th and 18th: The same wind; several thick fogs appeared. There were about four fingers of snow on the deck of the ship; this snow, which covers the masts and rigging, hardens through the night's cold; working the ship becomes extremely difficult. The weather is very distressing for the poor sailors, who are compelled during the very worst of the bad storms to climb the masts all wet and frozen to take in a reef, a piece of work which can only be carried out with bare hands. These men themselves were constantly soaked through in consequence of the waves which continually swept the deck.

On the 19th and 20th the weather remained overcast, with the very same wind as on the preceding days; frequent fogs; the days are very short in these regions. At mid-day the sun did not appear higher on the horizon than it is in Canada at eight o'clock in the morning in the month of March.

21st: Moderate wind, the sea a little calmer, weather clear and cold. We learned to-day that we had reached the 58° of South latitude, and that this is the line where we must double the Cape, which we are rapidly approaching. That is why we are indulging in the belief that we shall not much longer experience cold as severe as that we have already undergone, and that we shall soon see the end of that which caused so much distress. For far more than three months it had been impossible for us to remain upon the deck. Even though we visited there only through necessity, we experienced also many inconveniences in the between-decks where we lay. There was present a great humidity; the quarters were extremely cramped; a thick fog gathered as evening came on.

22nd: A good fresh wind, the weather cloudy. Light fogs during the day. We keep always to the 50° of latitude, and hope to arrive at the Cape within a very few days. I was surprised to see the planet Venus appear in the East round about eight o'clock in the evening, after having seen it set in the West at nightfall at the time of our departure from Sydney.

On the 23rd the wind rose, and from the look of the clouds it appeared as though it would continue for a long time; the sea exceedingly heavy; the water has rolled continually over the ship during the last two days. Today we reached this famous Cape, the terror of all mariners and travellers, the Cape so difficult to imagine and so impossible to describe. I had formed some idea of it from the narratives that I had read, and from the story told by certain travellers who had had the opportunity of visiting these shores, but, although I had believed the account exaggerated, it is, nevertheless, well below the reality, and not a single bit of what I have seen and heard was exaggerated. To give oneself some idea of these places, imagine a voyage below the 58° of South latitude, in the face of a continuous gale of violent wind, with rain and thick fog, a sea of which you would say that the waves rather fell from heaven than rolled upon the surface of the ocean, and ready to swallow you up every instant. In a word, to paint a picture of the sea in this region, imagine yourself surrounded by mountains of water moving ceaselessly and majestically.

26th and 27th: Strong westerly wind, overcast sky; rain and snow every now and then. We began to steer towards the N.E. while doubling the Cape, and this to our great satisfaction. For we hoped within a very few days to be freed from our miseries; that is to say, that we would be able to enjoy with greater comfort the benefit of remaining on deck when we came into warmer climates. Today about five o'clock the wind changed, blowing with force from the north. This compelled us to stand off the Cape.

28th: The wind was less fierce. It came from the west and blew us along in the right direction. The weather was fine, the sea very rough.

29th: Wind much the same as yesterday. We are making good progress, running to the N.E.

30th: Fine weather, wind west-south-west fairly strong. We are commencing to feel the first degrees of the heat of the Tropics as we advance to the North; it is a remarkable fact that two days after having doubled the Cape we became aware of a gradual but rapid change in the temperature.

31st: Cloudy weather, wind blowing from the west, but moderate enough.

1st September: Fine clear weather, westerly wind, fairly strong. We are forced to make a little more longitude than we would have wished, without, however, throwing ourselves off our course.

2nd and 3rd: Ever the same wind, coming, however, a little more from the north, and somewhat retarding our progress.

4th: Rainy weather; rather moderate southerly wind. It sent us along in a favourable direction. We had much latitude to make up. We have reached the 42° of South Latitude; we caught with the line several Cape Pigeons.

5th and 6th: Weather fine; very moderate south-west wind. Our stay on deck was pleasant. The weather had warmed up considerably since we began sailing north, although we have only as yet reached the 40° of South latitude.

7th and 8th: Weather overcast and rainy; a variable wind. Today, for the first time since our departure from Sydney, we were compelled to tack about. We have reached those parts where the winds arc variable throughout the whole course of the year. We saw a large number of dugongs around the ship today, as well as multitudes of birds. About ten o'clock the wind became favourable.

9th: Cloudy weather, westerly wind, a little contrary to our direction.

10th: A very violent wind blowing from the west-northwest. We were compelled to stand off the Cape for the whole day. The sea is extremely high, the weather rainy; we caught several birds. The tenth of each month has become for us a very notable date. Since our departure from Sydney this has been a day more or less noteworthy. It was on the 10th of July that we left the place of our exile; the 10th of August when we experienced a hurricane in the Eastern Pacific; and the 10th of September when we encountered another in the South Atlantic, or at any rate a wind of extraordinary fury, although it did not result in any accident.

11th and 12th: Strong westerly wind; weather serene and fairly warm; the sea very disturbed; we are making pretty fair progress. We saw many porpoises from fifteen to twenty feet long, and some even longer.

13th: Fine weather; wind west-north-west, fairly light. We learned that we had reached the 35° 14" of South latitude.

14th: Fine weather, wind decreased a little, the sea calm. We saw five or six whales during the course of the morning; some of them were very close to the ship. Towards ten o'clock in the morning we discovered on the horizon a sail, but it was hardly visible. A storm which blew up in the meantime hid it from us completely. Towards three o'clock p.m. the weather cleared and we saw the same sail. It was recognised as an American whaler named the *Tymar*. As it appeared to be approaching us, our Captain ran up a signal flag. But there was no reply at all; a little while afterwards, they directed their course directly towards us, and we passed under her stern. This was not only the first ship which we had met since our departure, but the very first object with the exception of birds and whales.

15th: Fine weather. It was already beginning to grow warmer - we learned that we were now in latitude 31° and longitude 34°.

16th: Fine weather; wind continues to be fresh but moderate. Cloudy weather in the afternoon.

17th: The wind turned south-west during the night. It was the first oncoming of the trade winds, which ought to reach us between the 28th and 30th degrees of latitude. These winds should consequently be very favourable to us as far as the same degree of North, latitude. To take advantage of these regular trade winds, we increased the number of our spars and sails.

18th and 19th: Fine weather, calm and very temperate. We commenced to suffer a little from the heat between decks, and especially at night. In the daytime we all stayed on deck, where we enjoyed the fresh air. We were most anxious for the wind so that we might pass through the Tropics as soon as possible, and advance still further on our journey.

20th: The sky serene; the sea calmer than I had ever seen it before. The atmosphere temperate. Towards mid-day, a very gentle westerly breeze sprang up.

21st: Weather fair, but warm; light breeze blowing from the west. We were in South latitude 29°.

22nd: Weather the same; wind coming from west-northwest, a little contrary to our direction.

23rd: Sky serene; the wind very strong and a little fresh. The ship is very uneasy. We saw flying fish for the first time since our departure. We have reached the 23° of South latitude.

On the 24th at six o'clock in the morning the wind changed from the southerly direction. The weather all day was overcast. This very day we passed Rio de Janeiro, but at a very great distance.

25th: Fairly strong southerly wind. The weather cloudy and rainy. Towards noon we catch sight of a sail on the horizon. We rapidly overtake this ship, which passes across our prow without any salute on either part. It is an American whaler called the *Elizabeth.*

26th: Light southerly wind; warm weather. We are in the 9th degree of South latitude.

27th: Some wind; cloudy sky. We suffered much from the heat, principally during the night, when it was almost impossible for us to sleep.

28th: Moderate south-east wind. The weather is warm. We now have in reality the trade winds, which blow from the south-east from April until November, as it has been stated at the beginning of this Journal. At nine o'clock the sky became covered with clouds, which presages one of those frequent dangerous storms which occur in the regions where we are. Happily it passed over without causing us anything but apprehension, and we experienced only a pleasant breeze.

27th: Weather overcast until nine o'clock in the morning, and then fine and warm. A light south-easterly breeze. We saw to-day for the first time since our departure a shark, which kept alongside the ship; while the crew was making preparations to catch it, it disappeared. We were now in latitude South 15° 30".

30th: Fine weather, but warm. We had now reached latitude South 15° 50". We met a Dutch ship bound for Batavia, one of the Indies. We greeted one another, and on account of the calm were in sight the whole day.

Ist October: Weather calm; the sea also smooth as ire, but keeping just one long majestic roll. The heat is excessive. It penetrates even into our quarters; we are very much inconvenienced by it. On the 2nd, to our great satisfaction, there blow a pleasant south-easterly breeze, which increased during the course of the day. This made up for our past sufferings. One of us caught in his hand a bird which came and rested on the bulwarks of the ship. On the 3rd it blew a fine southeast breeze. The heat was great; we were in latitude South 14° 8". On the 4th, the breeze stiffened during the night and blew violently. We advanced rapidly, making from six to seven miles an hour. We met a Scotch ship coming from Glasgow and steering for Bombay in the East Indies. The fierceness of the wind would not permit us to speak with it. We very soon lost sight of one another. Latitude 12° 24".

5th: The wind continued to blow from the south-east with force, and strongly favoured our progress. The weather was cloudy; we noticed that the wind was more constant since we reached 14° South latitude; we had in reality reached the region of the trade winds. Towards three o'clock ill the afternoon we met an American ship which was bound south. It came from Boston. We signalled one another. At eight o'clock in the evening we met another, which passed close by us. We could see it only very ill distinctly on account of the darkness. However, they held up a light quite a number of times. It is a somewhat remarkable occurrence that since we reached the Tropics all the birds, both small and great, which hitherto had surrounded our ship since the day of departure, gradually disappeared as we advanced towards the Equator, except, however, one species of little black and grey swallows that the English seamen call "Mother Carey's chickens."

On the 6th the wind continued in our favour with the same force, happily for us, for the sun darted its rays almost vertically on to our heads. Had it not been for the south-easterly breeze we should have suffered severely from the heat.

On the 7th the same wind, the sky cloudy and the weather warm. We passed to-day the solstitial point, which was then between South Latitude 5° 6" and Iongitude 29° 51" from Westminster. At some distance to the east we saw a ship.

On the 8th, the same wind, and a cloudless sky. We met an English brig coming from Jersey, bound for South America. We saw another at a great distance also making in the same direction. The weather was hot. Happily for us, the south-easterly breeze refreshed us. Latitude (South) 30°.

9th: Same wind, burning heat, cloudy sky. We saw hosts of flying fish and a large number of dugongs; the sailors tried to catch one of the latter. They did succeed in harpooning it; but at the very moment when they were about to pull it out of the water, the harpoon broke away, and the dugong, badly wounded though it was, escaped, reddening the water with its blood.

On the 10th October in the afternoon we passed the Equator on a fine day, somewhat refreshed by the feeble breeze. We were now at last in the Northern Hemisphere, our own, which we had left five years before. The sailors celebrated this day by a burlesque entertainment. They daubed one another with black; then they threw buckets of water over each other, so as to wash it off, as they said. They then put on fancy dresses, presented farces, sang songs, etc. But all this buffoonery was intended rather to obtain grog from the Captain than to show respect for Neptune. It is a custom on board all ships: sometimes even the passengers take part in the game.

On the 10th we had the same wind and the same weather as on preceding days. Between the Tropics the weather is very deceptive. The signs which indicate bad weather in our own country are often followed by fine weather and reciprocally. A peaceful sky is sometimes followed by violent squalls. It is easy enough for mariners to take precautions against them, for the cloud which produces them appears suddenly on the horizon, though sometimes it is very small. In then falls rapidly on the ship just like a thunderbolt, and tears away the rigging and the sails in spite of the precautions taken by the sailors. This is the fate that has been suffered by several ships whose crews did not have time to take precautions against these squalls: Frenchmen call this variety of clouds "Grains"; the English call it "White Squall." The heat had now become excessive. The sun was directly above our heads, and as the day declined its fierceness overcame us. One can easily get all idea of what we suffered between decks during the night. We could not sleep; sweat streamed over our bodies. Several of us were compelled to go and lie down on the deck, so as to try to get a little rest there. We met today three ships all bound south. They passed at a great distance from us.

On the 11th the wind had died down a little. It had become favourable to us, but on account of its lightness we advanced only slowly, We saw vast quantities of fish about the size of our mullet in Canada, These fish appeared to be amusing themselves on the surface of the sea, by leaping out of the water, Another somewhat remarkable fact is that after leaving the Tropic of Capricorn, as I have already noted, the birds had totally disappeared; now, however, a large number are to be found hovering above the fish of which I have just spoken, and who seem to follow their course, skimming along the surface of the water at whatever spot they show themselves, We do not know whether the birds carry out this performance so as to feed on these fish, an opinion which seems to me to be somewhat ill-founded, seeing that in size they do not exceed that of our domestic pigeons; nevertheless they had wings much longer. We had now reached Latitude 3° 35" North.

12th: The wind dropped almost entirely; the sky was overcast all day. Towards 2 o'clock p.m, a storm began to loom. The wind changed to easterly; but on the return to fine weather it resumed its former direction. For the first time I happened to go on deck barefooted, for, either through carelessness or some other reason, I had lost my slippers. To my great surprise I could not bear to stand on the deck. The heat of the sun had made it red hot, although the latter shone only at intervals; we suffered extremely from the heat,

13th: The weather is calm, the heat excessive. We saw several dolphins playing round the ship. These fish are very nimble. They turn and twist in every direction with incredible speed; they are about ten or twelve feet long. In the afternoon we saw two vessels, one to the south, the other to the north of us. They seemed to be on the same course as ourselves. During the night we had thunder and lightning.

14th: At six o'clock in the morning the weather was cloudy, and it commenced to rain almost immediately afterwards. During the day the wind blew up from the south-west, and became very strong until about five o'clock, when it died away almost entirely. We saw the same two ships that we had noticed the evening before; one was behind us and the other to the east. We took advantage of the rain which was falling to collect some water; we filled almost all our little vessels.

Although our ration was three litres daily, as we had to deduct therefrom the quantity necessary for our cooking, it was not sufficient, especially when we were between the Tropics, where it was necessary to be drinking continually, so as to quench our thirst and refresh ourselves. On the 15th the rain continued to fall copiously; the wind changed its direction several times in succession during the night; it even died right away and then sprang up again.

16th: Weather calm until 2 p.m., north-east wind. Suddenly there came a violent hurricane, accompanied by rain and thunder, which lasted about half an hour; a calm of about an hour succeeded, then the breeze sprang up again. We were in Latitude 9° North. The night was fairly pleasant.

17th: Rainy weather the whole day. The wind changed direction several times during the course of the day. A deep calm always followed storms.

18th: The weather had become fair, the sky serene, the wind north-east. We believed that this wind was the Trade Wind or the Monsoon which had reappeared.

19th: Same wind as yesterday; the sky clear. We saw many dugongs, some whales, and flying fish in multitudes. These N.E. winds refreshed us greatly, because we found them very delightful after having endured the heat of the Equator, which had caused us so much distress.

20th: The wind continued to blow from the same quarter with a little more force, which compelled us to make a little more westerly longitude than was advantageous to us. Towards seven o'clock in the evening the sky became covered with thick clouds, the wind grew very wild, and the sea much disturbed, we were almost on a parallel with the Cape Verde Islands, 14° 3" North.

21st: The north-easter continues to blow with much violence; the sea is terrible; the waves frequently hurl themselves over the deck. We had never seen the sea in such a disturbed state since Cape Horn. Latitude 16° North.

22nd: Same weather as on preceding days; the sea is much rougher than usual; the violence of the wind is such that several sails have been torn and put out of service; the spars themselves even showed signs of breaking. Latitude 18° North. Towards five o'clock in the evening, we met a brig which passed to the east of us, and appeared to be bound for the South Pacific.

23rd: The wind blows with the same impetuosity, the sky is cloudy, the sea very rough, the waves swamp the ship frequently during the course of the day. We are in latitude 20° 7" North.

24th: The wind had subsided a little, but it continued to blow from the same quarter; the sky is cloudless. Towards eight o'clock in the morning we met a vessel bound for the West Indies. Round about four o'clock we caught sight of another ahead of us. Latitude 22° 50".

25th: Same north-east wind, but very moderate, blowing always in a favourable direction. We had in sight two vessels on the same course as ourselves. One of them had been through a tempest and had its top fore-masts and its mainmasts broken off, a disaster which had nearly happened to us a few days ago. Latitude 27° North.

26th: Absolutely calm weather the whole day long.

27th: The wind blew gently from the north-east until one p.m. after which the wind increased and constrained us to work the ship. In the course of the afternoon several squalls broke violently over us. We were of opinion that we had left the Trade winds and had caught up with the variable winds again. Latitude 27° North.

28th: The wind coming from the same direction and with the same force, we were blown far from our course.

29th: Same wind as yesterday. We saw much seaweed upon the surface of the sea. It came from the Gulf of Mexico and Florida, carried along by the currents and the westerly winds which prevails in these parts.

30th: The wind had moderated a little, although blowing always from the same quarter. We saw two ships a great distance away.

31st: The sky was covered the whole day with thick clouds. The wind is very variable.

1st November: Weather calm all day. Towards evening the horizon was darkened by black clouds. We anticipated a storm almost immediately. Latitude 32° N., longitude 35" West.

2nd: At six o'clock in the morning the breeze blew gently from the south-west, and gradually increased until mid-day, when it blew strongly, and consequently was favourable to us. Two ships passed across our bows, making for the East; one of the two was American.

3rd: The wind ever continued to blow with the same force. The sky was overcast and threatened a storm. To our great satisfaction, we discussed the possibility of our arriving in London in fewer than twelve days, if the wind did not cease to be favourable. It is not necessary to say that we were in need of refreshment, and that we were extremely fatigued with the journey. Several of us showed symptoms of scurvy. We have reached 34° North Latitude.

4th: At six o'clock in the morning the wind suddenly changed to a fierce north-easter, and blew contrary to our course; the weather rainy, and the sea very rough.

5th: The same wind as yesterday continued to blow with the same force, although it had veered a little from the east. The weather was overcast. Latitude 36° 30".

6th: East-north-east wind, and blowing us along in the right direction; weather overcast and rainy. We saw two brigs. We approached one of them and spoke to her. She was an English brig named *Adina-Dundee,* hailing from Glasgow. The cold began to make itself felt. We were in latitude 38° North.

7th: Same wind as yesterday. Weather serene. Towards night, it was only by a narrow margin that a collision between our ship and the vessel that we had seen the evening before was averted. About six o'clock in the evening she was only a short distance away from us. We came much closer still in the darkness of the night, when suddenly we were surprised to see that only a space of about twenty rods separated us. Latitude 39° 40" North.

8th: Towards four o'clock in the morning the wind changed to the south-east, and brew fiercely. It was in our favour. We left the Azores Islands on our east; the sky was cloudless, and the weather fresh, Latitude 41° 4".

9th: Wind changed to the south-west in the course of the night, and was still favourable to us, since we had to make more longitude than latitude. An English barque caught up with us; we approached and spoke to it. It was on its way from Valparaiso (Chili) and was called *Orator-London.* It was one hundred and twenty days out, and, like ourselves, had doubled Cape Horn. Longitude 34° West.

10th: The wind blew west-south-west with considerable force, and carried us along on a favourable course. Latitude 42° North, longitude 62° West.

11th: The wind increased and blew pretty strongly. The sea was very rough. It was covered with foam white as snow. We made eight miles an hour. Today the sailors got the anchors ready, hoping, if the wind lasted, for an early arrival in London. We were all delighted to see that the wind was so favourable to us and were very anxious to set foot on shore again. For one hundred and twenty-five days we had seen the land only once. We were extremely weary of the voyage, especially during the last few days, our food having been reduced to salt beef of very poor quality, and to weevily biscuit.

12th: It rained the whole day; the weather was overcast and foggy, the sea very rough.

13th: The breeze came from the south-west and blew fairly regularly; the weather was dull and misty. We met a ship making her way west; we steered due east. Latitude 44°, North, longitude 24° West.

14th and 15th: Weather rainy, with a strong south-west wind still favourable to us, for we were steering due east into the mouth of the English Channel. We saw several vessels during these last two days. Towards eight o'clock in the evening, as the night was dark and rainy, we almost collided with a ship which came head on to us in full sail. The impact would have been terrible and would have been the destruction of one or other of the vessels. Fortunately the other ship caught sight of us and hoisted a lantern. An officer of our crew was reduced in rank for having failed to place a sentry in the bow of the ship, as he had been ordered to do.

16th: The weather changed; the sky cleared and the wind moved a few points to the south. Latitude 48° 30", longitude 13° 30" West.

17th: The sky was covered with thick clouds, and the wind, blowing from the south-east, was a little against us. The weather was fresh; we saw many birds, the presence of which we had not noticed for a long time. That convinced us that we were not far from land: we even thought that we were within the Channel itself.

18th: Cloudy weather; strong south-west wind blowing. We discovered, to our great satisfaction, that we were within the entrance to the Channel. We were delighted with the thought that inside four or five days we would be able to set foot on shore. We saw several ships and a great number of diving ducks around us. The first point of English land which came into our view was Lizard Point, at the southern extremity of England. We made rapid progress during the night.

19th: Towards nine o'clock we were suddenly assailed by the cry of "Land! Land! "We saw the land on our port side. It was Start Point, which we passed at some little distance. The day was a happy one for all of us, and everything contributed to increase our delight. The weather was fine, and a light and favourable breeze bowled us along rapidly towards our destination. This particular day we had for dinner some fresh pork which the crew had prepared the evening before. It goes without saying that we found this food delicious, not having tasted any fresh meat for a hundred and thirty days, and being deprived for a whole month even of salt pork. On all sides we saw ships coming and going, and principally many small boats engaged in the coastal trade between England and France. One of them came alongside and offered us some fish. Of these, amongst other kinds, I noticed one variety that they call "Garnet." These fish were red, of a peculiar shape and excellent for eating. Our captain made a bargain with them to take off the mail. It cost him thirty shillings, an amount that he paid with tobacco, salt beef, tea and rum. One of the cabin passengers went ashore on the same boat.

On the 20th we had splendid weather, though it was cloudy.

The wind was fresh and favourable. We had the pleasure of seeing the Isle of Wight, which appeared to be very lofty; we also saw many ships. A boat came alongside us with a pilot, but he had nothing to do with us, seeing that he was not licensed to pilot ships going to ports other than those of the Isle of Wight, to which station he was attached. In the course of the night we passed Beachy Head, where there is a lighthouse.

21st: Another glorious day, fresh and calm, although the wind was against us. We did not see land until about eleven o 'clock in the morning.

This was Dungeness, which is a long point of level sand, upon which was erected a brick lighthouse. We also distinguished Hastings, which is a small town to the south of Dungeness. We saw an unusual number of ships moving about from one side to the other. Today we again saw the pilot who was to bring us in to Dover. In the course of the evening we caught sight on the east of us of a fine lighthouse that we were told was a French lighthouse built just a little previously. We learned from the pilot that the barque *Jane Goudie* had passed here exactly six days before us, all occurrence which is remarkable after so long a voyage. This meant in effect that the rate of progress of the two ships must have been exactly the same for one not to have beaten the other by even so much as *one* day. We noticed that the water of the Channel was green. I do not know the cause of this: whether it is the natural colour of the water, or whether it is produced by the bed of the current, or by other causes. Some Dutch sloops passed by us. We came to all anchor a little below Dungeness.

22nd: At six o'clock in the morning we raised our anchor. A strong contrary breeze was blowing. It was only by tacking from side to side that we could make a little progress. Towards nine o'clock in the morning we caught sight of the cliffs of Dover, which are cut perpendicularly to the sea and white as snow. They are in reality composed of chalk or white plaster. We came closer in and saw Dover at the head of a little bay. It appeared to us to be a small town, stylishly built, and surrounded by the white cliffs of which I have just spoken. There is also upon one of the cliffs near the town a splendid castle, and a little distance away a lighthouse; and some broad fields which extend to the north-west, and which appeared to us well cultivated. Everyone knows the antiquity of this town and how many memories are linked up with it. It is there that landed the great army which brought chains to the Britons hitherto proud and free; which laid down the road for those hordes of fierce barbarians who in successive waves spread over British soil, and reddened it with blood. From when we were, we could easily discover Calais on the French coast, situated exactly opposite Dover. We all felt quite an emotional thrill when we saw the country of our ancestors. In a little time we arrived opposite Deal, another little town seven or eight miles from Dover, situated on a flat and sandy area of land. As the wind was contrary and the tide against us, we dropped our anchor in front of the town, where we could observe it at our convenience, it contains only eight thousand inhabitants, whose principal occupation is fishing. This place is famous as the spot where Julius Caesar made his descent on England at the time of his first expedition into this country. We had now reached the Dunes, dangerous localities, on account of the number of sand banks which, on all sides, obstruct the passage of ships; in addition, shipwrecked vessels are frequently to be seen here. The bottom is composed of shifting sand, as a consequence of which from day to day the tide forms these banks, which are impassable, and which move about from place to place. There is a steamer hired by the Government to work over arid sound this locality every day, so as to discover the sand banks and to mark them down. We saw this vessel cross and re-cross in various directions, and a number of buoys placed here and there, as well as some light-ships. A number of boats came alongside us with fish, bread, apples, etc. The seashores of this part of England are fairly smooth and level, I noticed that the accounts given us concerning the smoky atmosphere which obscures the sky of England were quite true, and that the cause of it was the immense quantity of coal which is consumed in the innumerable factories which exist there. Besides, all the villages and all the towns that we saw were covered with smoke.

23rd: At nine o'clock in the morning we came to an anchor in the mouth of the Thames. We could not advance farther on account of the ebbing tide, which was forming currents strong enough to drag us on to some sand banks which, as I have already said, are very common hereabouts. Several steamboats passed near us, on their way to France, Holland and various other places. Several ships came and anchored close to us, awaiting the following day's tide. We anchored at a depth of 22 feet of water at low tide, on a sandy bottom. We were opposite Margate and Ramsgate.

24th: At six o'clock in the morning we raised anchor, and, favoured by a slight breeze as well as by the flowing tide, we had soon reached the mouth of the Thames on the south shore. We saw many large warships lying here and there. We tied up to a steamer, which towed us as far as Gravesend, where we anchored again to wait for the tide, for the ebb and flow are so strong in the Thames that it is difficult to move against the current. Gravesend is a rather pretty little town in a good position. An officer came and took up his position on board, so as to see that there should be no smuggling during our voyage to London. We also changed our pilot; the Captain of our ship went ashore with several passengers. At eight o'clock in the evening we raised our anchor once more, and a steamer towed us up to. London. The banks of the Thames are, generally speaking, fairly low and of good appearance. We anchored in the Pool of London at midnight. We spent five days in London strolling about and seeking a passage for one or other of the ports of the United States, since the season was too far advanced, for ships to pass through the Gulf of St. Lawrence.

I shall give no detailed account of London, since it is too well known; I shall limit myself merely to the statement that it is very difficult to conceive the extent of English trade. To get an idea of it, one must see the immense warehouses crammed with goods, both foreign and home produced; the merchant marine, of which ships of every tonnage line both sides of the Thames from its mouth right up to London, a distance of about thirty miles; as well as the vast docks which have been built in London and its vicinity. The imports and exports which take place in London every day, to tell the truth, reach an almost incredible total. Although I had already known London by renown, I confess that I had only a very imperfect idea of it, and that I was astonished when I saw it. I could not bring myself to the belief that there could exist so great a commercial city. He who has not seen London cannot imagine what it is like. As we were not able to remain more than a few days in the city, we employed the time that we had seeing the places and buildings of greatest interest, such as Covent Garden, which is a place of splendid walks; St. Paul's Cathedral, so famous. for its size and antiquity; the Stock Exchange or "Royal Exchange"; the Tower and the numerous public buildings; the Palace and several magnificent edifices belonging to the Government and to some of the nobility; and in addition the monuments, the public squares, the bridges, and that which we found most astonishing of all - the "Tunnel," as the English call it. This is an underground road, as is well known to everyone, excavated beneath the Thames, and twelve hundred feet in length, above which pass ships and steamers. When we were within it, to our great surprise we could hear the noise made by these vessels. This underground passage is illuminated day and night by gas. Fruit and other refreshments are sold there. A fee of one penny is charged for admission. Before arriving at the platform upon which the road is built, one must descend sixty odd feet by means of an escalator. I think that I ought here to say a word concerning our situation in London. The reader, knowing how much it was a subject of criticism, will better appreciate the kindness which was shown to us there, and will give to its author the tribute of a recognition that he deserves.

When we left Sydney, after making an estimate of the cost of our return to our homes, we well knew that our means were insufficient to take us there, and that we could not proceed farther than London. This difficulty did not deter us: for we hoped that, once having reached this town, whether by our own work or by the help that we might be able to receive from our fellow-countrymen, or by some lucky chance, we would ultimately reach the end of our journey. We found ourselves, then, without resources in London, strangers, unknown; and we did not know how to extricate ourselves from this predicament.

In ordinary circumstances, an interesting experience often makes but a feeble impression on the mind, and the memory of it soon fades away; but if misfortune overtakes you, then it comes back, and with a vividness quite fresh. We profited by this benevolent attention of Providence. While our unhappy thoughts beset us, the thought of Mr. Roebuck suddenly came back to our minds. We recalled with tender feelings that on more than one occasion he had shown kindness to our compatriots, and we believed that his generous heart would become interested in our misfortunes. We decided, therefore, to approach him by way of a letter, and this is what one of us, M. Lanctôt,[26] wrote to him:-

John Roebuck[27] Esq. London, 28th December, 1844
M.P. etc. etc.

Sir,

A recent arrival in this Capital, a nameless stranger, without credit, without any other recommendations except his misfortunes, would much like to aspire to the favour of communicating with you. A victim of the political disturbances of which his country, Canada, was recently afflicted, it is on account of the patriotism with which he early associated your name that he now dares take the liberty of submitting to your consideration the following short statement of his situation.

Banished from his native land, kept in subjection for more than six years, he has at last regained his freedom, together with those of his fellow countrymen who shared with him the same fate. It was in June last that he received the news of his recall. This release, however tardy, he appreciates, and congratulates himself on it; he has henceforth the tender hope of seeing once again all that which binds him most dearly to the world, his native land, his wife, his relatives, his friends. But he cannot yet enjoy his good fortune; it is only an expectation; there remain to him limitless seas to be crossed, an expensive voyage to undertake, and he is without resources, without means, and the majority of his fellow countrymen in exactly the same position. Sydney could offer only a difficult existence to these strangers; when they received their pardons, it was not until the year '42 that they were permitted to live in their own houses; until that time they had been detained in a penal, establishment. Their anxiety is extreme; weary, worn almost to exhaustion by the miseries and privations of a long captivity; always present in their thoughts, the picture of their wives and their children suffering the anguish of being separated from them; they are impatient to leave places where they never experienced anything except irritations and vicissitudes. However, this painful state of indecision ought not to be of long duration. A letter from Canada has reached one of the exiles; it, tells us that our friends have forseen our situation and our needs, and that they have to the raising of certain funds to assist our return home. In the position in which we found ourselves, we took counsel with one another concerning our respective means; those who had the most extended the hand to those who had less, and finally we arrived at a total of 38 who were in a state sufficient to enable them to take passage for England, and we left Sydney once and for all on the

10th of July last, and at the end of a four and a half months' voyage reached this land; always under the impression that the funds and cash in question would have reached there before us, and that they would have been addressed to the care of one who has always been the devoted friend of all Canadians, the acknowledged defender of their cause.

There remains nothing more than to ask your pardon for my extreme boldness in writing to you, and to beg you to believe that I will appreciate any information with which you may be pleased to honour me, as I as well as my companions should do.

I have the honour to be, &c., HPT. LANCTOT

As everyone knows, the response was the assistance which Mr. Roebuck rendered us by procuring for us the wherewithal to continue our voyage. As a result :-

29th November, we embarked on board the American ship *Switzerland,* of six [hundred] tons burthen, sailing for New York under the command of Captain Knight. At six o'clock p.m. we left St. Catherine's dock, and were towed by a steamer which was to take us out of the Thames. As night was coming on, we cast anchor a little this side of Gravesend; this circumstance gave us the opportunity of seeing that part of the Thames which lies between London and the mouth of the river, for on our course up we had made this journey at night. We had the pleasure of seeing Greenwich, through which passes the Meridian line, and which possesses a splendid military hospital built on the banks of the Thames. One can say that London begins at this spot, for from this point as far as London the buildings, factories, as well as private houses, form one continuous chain.

30th: We anchored opposite Margate, the wind being contrary and the passage difficult. By reason of the number of sandbanks which obstruct the entrance to the Thames we could not go any further.

1st December: We raised anchor at daylight in the morning, and tacked about the whole day so as to avoid the sandbanks. Early in the evening we dropped anchor, for we had to contend against both wind and tide. The weather was cold and wet.

2nd: We tacked again the whole day without being able to make much headway. In the evening we were opposite Ramsgate. We were fairly close to the shore. This place, situated on the extremity of a point of land which stretches out into the Channel, appeared to us of somewhat attractive appearance.

3rd: The wind proving favourable, we left the Dunes and arrived at Portsmouth about four o'clock in the afternoon. We did not cast anchor. The captain and some passengers came on board in a boat. We could not see the port, which is very extensive, and which contains many warships. We had only a distant view of the town, but according to the account which Lanctot gave us of it, it is divided into three parts, handsomely built, and contains eighty thousand people. Lanctot had journeyed to Portsmouth overland by railway, having been detained in London on business which does not concern us.

4th: We had a favourable wind; we saw Start Point as we passed by. In the evening the wind fell; we still had the land in sight, but at a great distance.

5th: We had lost sight of land; the wind was favourable; we made rapid progress towards America. The weather was fresh and the sky overcast.

6th: The wind continued fair the whole day; the weather was cloudy, but fine.

7th: The breeze grew stronger and blew constantly from the north-east; we made nine or ten knots an hour.

8th: The wind was very fierce, and the sea almost as wild; the water came aboard every minute, although the ship was big and very high out of the water. Many of us became ill, as much from seasickness as from cold in the head. The wind fell during the course of the night.

9th: The weather was calm all day; the sea very rough. We had the pleasure of watching a whale at our leisure; it played round the ship for at least two hours, appearing quite close to us every minute or so.

10th: The wind was violent, blowing from the north-west, but unfavourable to our route.

11th: The same wind, but much moderated; weather overcast and stormy; we tacked all day.

12th: During the night the wind rose to a furious height; the sea became so wild that on the ship everything was overturned-boxes, pots and pans, furniture, etc. The waves battered the ship as though she had crashed against a rock; the water poured down in torrents into the between-decks through the hatchway; the wind and the sea set up a dreadful moaning; it grew cold; it hailed. Daylight at last appeared, showing us the sea in a fury such as we had not seen it since Cape Horn. To put the finishing touch to our misfortunes, the wind was south-west, and contrary to our course, which compelled us to hove to close to the wind as possible.

13th: The same wind persisted; the sea always as heavy; the ship rocked horribly; several people were laid up through seasickness. The sky foreboded wind.

14th: The same wind continued with the same force; we met a small brig sailing to the East. It was really curious to see this little vessel so tossed about by the sea; although it was but a little distance away from us, we lost sight of it every instant, only to see it to appear again as though on a mountain peak, at one time on its side, at another time either with prow or stern in air. One would have said it was a bit of cork on the surface of the water.

15th: The wind blew constantly with force from the northwest. We passed within sight of the Azores, some little distance away. They are a group of very high islands, inhabited by the Portuguese. They produce a great abundance of fruits and enjoy a delightful climate, although they are subject to earthquakes. Fayol is the chief port, and Agra the capital of these islands. The port is perfectly safe. These islands are situated in 40° N. Latitude and 30° E. Longitude, almost half-way between New York and Europe.

16th: The weather was calm and cloudy the whole day. Later it had greatly improved and showed signs of wind.

17th: The breeze had increased a little, corning from the south-west; that is to say, contrary to our course, so that it was necessary to tack the whole day.

18th: Same wind as yesterday. We saw a ship making north-east. With the oncoming of the evening, the wind became fierce; the sea was very disturbed the whole night long. The sky was clear and the air mild.

19th: The wind blew constantly from the south-west with some force; the sea was rough. Every moment waves swamped the ship;

several of us were much affected by seasickness, myself especially. Towards evening the wind completely, died away, and the sky became clouded; we were all sorry to see the wind always contrary to our route, we who so ardently desired to return to the bosoms of our families and who were so tired of sea travelling. Everything combined to make us find the days long and tedious; however, we still had another fortnight's journey ahead.

20th, 21st, 22nd: The wind blew eyer strongly from the south-west; the air and the weather both cold.

23rd: The weather was calm, except for a light southwesterly breeze. We passed a large quantity of seaweed which came from the Gulf of Florida. We were now on the same parallel as the south-eastern extremity of the Banks of Newfoundland. We saw a variety of little birds about the size of a nightingale flying round the ship and plunging into the water. We met a Danish vessel making north-east; it exchanged signals with us.

24th: About midnight the wind gradually rose from the east-south-east, a direction favourable to our course. At eight o 'clock in the morning it blew violently; we made eleven knots an hour on a direct course; this caused us much pleasure, as we had been so long opposed by the west winds since leaving the Channel. We hope soon to be in New York.

But on the 25th the wind blew from the west, to make us, as it were, atone for our satisfaction of the previous evening. The weather was cold and the sky clouded.

26th and 27th: The wind varied from south-west to north-west; weather clear and cold; the sea very rough.

28th: The wind fell entirely; during the night it rained.

Towards ten o'clock in the morning a breeze sprang up from the east in a favourable direction, arousing once again the hope of our soon seeing land. We were now at the northern end of the Banks of Newfoundland.

29th: The wind died down about midnight; we also had rain. The whole day was calm. We cast fishing lines into the water, for, being on the Banks of Newfoundland, we thought we might catch some cod. We saw many ducks and several whales.

30th: The wind blew fiercely from the north; the weather cold and overcast.

31st: Variable winds arid cloudy weather.

1st January, 1845: This day of happiness for Canada was for us a very sad one, for we had been tricked by the weather. We had calculated that we would have arrived by New Year's Day at the very latest, and we had anticipated a fine welcome celebration. Nevertheless, we knew that our relatives must be awaiting us with anxiety, for they must have received news of our departure from London by the steamer which was due to leave Liverpool four days after us, and to arrive at New York twelve or fifteen days before us. In the meantime we spent the day as well as it was possible. We procured some brandy from the Captain of the ship and celebrated the good old times he had had in Canada, encouraged by the prospect which we had of soon reaching the end of our miseries and fatigues, and of once more setting foot on our native soil. The weather was calm the whole day; towards evening the south-west breeze sprang up as usual.

2nd: The wind continued to blow from the south-west; the weather cold and cloudy. We met two ships.

3rd: The wind blew with some force; the sea was terribly rough. It hailed and snowed the whole day and became very cold. We noticed that we had become very sensitive to the cold, a circumstance little surprising, after our having inhabited warm climates for five years. We passed a fearful night.

Nothing is more terrible than to see a stormy night; a violent wind accompanied by hail and snow whistling in the rigging; the waves, swollen and red as fire, breaking every moment over the vessel. When day broke the wind fell.

4th: Weather calm until mid-day; suddenly the heavens grow dark, and a minute later a frightful storm bursts; the waves wash the deck. The main topsail flies into ribbons, as does another sail; the rigging gives way everywhere. Violent shocks shake the vessel's timbers; the same wind as the previous night. Never was a crossing from London to New York more difficult. Since we left the Channel we have had only two days' fair wind. However, despite the south-west and northwest winds which generally prevail at this season of the year, we calculate that we shall reach New York this very week.

5th: A light south-westerly wind; sky cloudy; during the night a sharp storm, accompanied by snow; at daylight, calm weather. For the last fortnight the wind has been contrary, or the weather calm.

6th: Calm until mid-day, then a contrary north-westerly wind; weather cloudy.

7th: During the night the wind sprang up with furious violence from the east. Consequently we made direct progress towards the shores of America. At eight o'clock in the morning the wind was so strong that we were compelled to shorten sail; except for the topsail, the foresail and the trysail, and even in the latter, reefs had to be taken, otherwise an accident would have happened. Thus the wind lasted until mid-day, when it suddenly changed to the south-west, which made the sea terribly disturbed. It rained, and the whole day was very foggy.

8th: The wind north-west, fairly strong, and absolutely contrary to our course. The weather cold and overcast. We took soundings; there were twenty-five fathoms of water. About four o'clock in the afternoon we met three ships all bound north-east.

9th: The weather was calm until nine o'clock; then a light breeze from the south-west sprang up; the weather was cold, but fine. We expect to see land to-morrow.

10th: Wind north-west; weather clear and cold. About nine o'clock, to our great content, we heard the cry, "Land! Land!" Then we saw ahead of us a shore upon which we could make out some buildings. It was Black Island, situated on the east side of Long Island. But the contrary wind prevented us from coming closer in, and we were compelled to tack to the south-west. We did not see the land again the whole of that day. The whole night was calm and rainy. We all felt great delight at seeing the land, after a journey so long and so painful as that we had had since leaving London, and at that gentle hope that filled us of soon reaching the end of our distressful voyage and of returning to the midst of our families.

12th: Early in the morning we were told that a lighthouse was visible straight ahead, and as soon as day dawned we made out the coast, which was that of New Jersey, and that we were running along the shore as far as Sandy Hook, where we anchored, while waiting for a steamer which was to come and tow us to New York. To be exact, the tugboat took us in tow at 3 p.m. But the wind rising so strong and so contrary, and the tide being against us, we were compelled to anchor at the extremity of Sandy Hook and to cast off the tugboat, which was to come and take us in tow again the following morning, Sandy Hook is a delightful sandy beach, upon which are several fine lighthouses. From this place the view of the neighbouring shores is enchanting, not only on account of the beauty of the site itself, but also of the splendour of the buildings. We saw some little spots of snow along the fences.

13th: Early in the morning the tugboat returned and towed us right into the port, where we disembarked round about ten o'clock. We had the pleasure of seeing several of our Canadian friends, who had come to meet us on the Quay. It was the first time that we had seen any Canadians since our departure from Canada, and for the first time also since we set foot on American soil. We already began to think of our return to Canada. On setting foot on shore, our first thought was for our benefactors, so M. Lanctôt, in our name, addressed to Mr. Fabre the following letter, to thank all the generous folk who had contributed to the expenses of our return to our native land :-

To Mr. E. R. Fabre.

New York, 15th January, 1845.

Allow me to take the liberty of addressing to you a few words, which my actual position in certain. respects seems to permit me to do. I wish however to take up as little of your time as possible. We have just arrived here, myself and thirty seven other political exiles. The copy of a letter that we addressed to Mr. Roebuck, at the time of our short stay in London, and which I have the honour to attach herewith, will tell you enough of our situation and will acquaint you fairly well with the details of what we have done in connexion with this gentleman, and of the causes and motives which compelled us to take this course; I have not the slightest doubt that Mr. Roebuck has written to you on this matter before I have been able to do so, and that you already know what this noble friend has deigned to do for us on this occasion. Nevertheless, I cannot let the opportunity pass without expressing a word or two of thanks myself, nor allowing any time to elapse before giving expression to the feelings of gratitude which have possessed not only myself but also my compatriots on account of the very real help that you and a great number of other true friends have so generously provided for the accomplishment of our return from exile.

Be so good, therefore, to accept, Sir, the humble thanks of all these gentlemen.

I am, with all possible respect,
Your very humble and most obedient servant,

HPT. LANCTOT

Some business matters kept us for two days in New York. This town is so well known that I may be spared the necessity of describing it.

15th: In the morning we took passage on a steamer which landed us at Bridgeport, whence we journeyed to Albury, where we slept that night. The following morning at six o'clock we took the stage coach, passing through Castle Town, Middleberry, Virgin, Burlington, etc. On the 18th we arrived at St. Jean. and the following day separated to rejoin our families after an absence of five years and a half. We had taken six months and nine days to return from exile to Canada.

Registered in accordance with the Provincial Act,
29th September, 1845.

FRENCH-CANADIAN PRISONERS

Arrived by the Ship "Buffalo," 1840.

Alerie, Michael, 38 Joiner.
Bechard, Theodore, 49 Farmer and veterinary surgeon Bergevin, Charles, (Charles Langevin the elder] 53 Farmer Bigonnesse, F'rancois, (dit Beaucaire) 49, Farmer
Bouc, Guillaume Charles, 46, Clerk
Bourbonnais, Desire, 20 Blacksmith
Bourdon, Louis, 23 farmer and Merchant's Clerk
Bousquet, Jean Baptiste, 44 Farmer and Miller
Buisson, Constant, 30 Blacksmith
Chevrefils, Gabriel Ignace, 43 Farmer
Coupal, Antonie, (dit La Reine), 50 Farmer
Desfayettes, Louis, 49 Farmer
Ducharme, Leon, *(alias* Léandro Ducharme), 23 Merchant's Clerk
Dumouchelle, Joseph, 47 farmer
Dumouchelle, Louis Guerin, *(alias* Blanc Dusalt), 37 Farmer
Gagnon, David, 29 Joiner and Carpenter
Goyette, Jacques, 49 Mason and Farmer
Goyette, Joseph, 29 Carpenter
Guerin, Louis, 36 Farmer
Guertin, Francois, 44 Carpenter and Joiner
Guimond, Joseph, 48 Carpenter and Farmer
Hébert, Jacques David [alias David Jacques Hébert], 49 Farmer
Hébert, Joseph Jacques, 42 Farmer
Huot, Charles, 53 Notary public
Laberge, Jean, 36 Farmer
Lanctot, Hypolite, 23 Notary public
Langlois, Etienne, 26 Farmer
Languedoc, Etienne, 22 Farmer
Lavoie, Pierre. 49 Farmer
Leblanc, David Drossin, 36 Farmer
Lepailleur, Francois Maurice, 33 House painter
Longtin, Jacques, 59 Farmer
Longtin, Moyse (son of Jacques), 24 Farmer

Marceau, Joseph, (alias Petit Jacques), 34 Farmer and weaver
Morin, Achille, 25
Morin, Hector Pierre, 54 Clerk
Mott, Benjamin, 43 Mariner
Newcombe, Samuel, 65 Farmer
Papineau, André, (dit Montigny), Surgeon and blacksmith Pare, Joseph, 48
Pinsonnault, Louis, 40 Farmer
Pirisonnault, Rene,48 Farmer
Pinsonnault, Paschal, 27 Farmer
Prevost, François Xavia, 30 Farmer
Prieur, François Xavier, 24 Merchant
Robert, Théophile, 25 Merchant
Rochon, Toussaint, 30 Farmer
Rochon, Edouard Paschal, 39 Carriage maker and painter
Rochon, Jeremie, 36 Carriage maker and painter
Roy, Basile, 49 Wheelwright
Roy, Charles, (dit Lapensée the elder)
Roy, Joseph, (dit Lapensée fils de Louis), 52 Farmer
Thibert, Jean Louis, 52 Farm labourer
Thibert, Jean Marie, 38 Farm labourer
Touchette, François Xavier, 32 Blacksmith and farmer
Trundelle, Jean Baptiste, 34 Farmer and joiner
Turcot, Louis, 36 Farmer

END NOTES

1. For the trials, see *Report of the State Trials Before a General Court-Martial, held at Montreal in* 1838-9. Two volumes. Montreal, Armour and Ramsay, 1839.

2. See *Report of the State. Trials,* Vol.1 p.17.

3. One hundred and eight men were tried, twelve were executed, nine acquitted, fifty-eight transported, the remainder liberated on bail, See *Report of the State Trials,* Vol. H, Appendix.

For ampler details of the Rebellion, the reader is referred to the following

L. O. David: *Les Pairiot es de 1837-1838.* Montreal, 1884.

A.E. Decelles: *The "Patriotes" of '37.* Toronto, 1916.

E.C. Guillet: *The Lives and Timesof the Patriots.* Toronto, 1938.

Report of the Earl of Durham. New Edition. London 1902.

E. A. Theiler: *Canada in 1837-8.* Two volumes. Philadelphia, 1841.

J. D. Barnett: "The Books of the Political Prisoners and Exiles of 1838," in *Papers and Records of the Ontario Historical Society,* Vol. XVI. Toronto, 1918.

F. H. Severance : "Literature of the Upper Canada Rebellion," in *Publications of the Buffalo Historical Society,* Vol. V. Buffalo, 1902.

References to the French-Canadian "Patriots" will also be found scattered through the following Narratives, written by prisoners from Upper Canada, transported in the *Buffalo* to Van Dieman's Land, who also returned to their native land :-

Gates, William: *Recollections of Life in Van Diemen's Land.* Lockport, 1850.

Wright, Stephen: *Narrative and Recollections during a Three Years' Captivity* (written by Caleb Lyon). New York, 1844.

Miller, Linus B.: *Notes of an Exile in Van Diemen's Land.* New York, 1846.

Wait, James: *Van Diemen's Land, written during Four Years' Imprisonment.* Buffalo, 1843.

Marsh, Robert: *Seven Years of My Life, or a Narrative of a Patriotic Exile.* Buffalo, 1847.

Snow, Samuel: *The Exile's Return, or Narrative of Samuel Snow.* Cleveland, 1846.

Heustis, Daniel D.: *A Narrative of the Adventures and Sufferings of Captain Daniel D. Heustis.* Boston, 1847.

4. Eighty-three prisoners, after the Rebellion in Upper Canada were, transported to Van Diemen's Land. See Guillet: *The Lives and Times of the Patriots,* chaps. XX. and XXI.

5. In my possession is a MS. document headed "A Rule for Victualling the Hulks *Fortune* and *Ceres* in Langston Harbour, 1790," which sets out the Convicts' Ration Rate as under:-

"Breakfast for a Mess of Six men: Five quarts and one pint of Soup made of Barley and Oatmeal.

"SUNDAY.- Dinner for Mess of Six Men: Six Pounds of Salt Beef with 4 lb Potatoes, six pounds of Biscuit and five Quarts Small Beer.

"MONDAY.- Six pounds fresh Beef with 4 lb Potatoes and Two Loaves 4 lb each to them that work on shore and for them on board a loaf of six pounds.

"TUESDAY.- Two Pounds and a half of Cheese. Bread as above, and similarly to Monday and Tuesday on alternate week-days.

"SUNDAY.-*Supper*: Five quarts and one pint of Soup made of Barley Meal and Greens, or of Burgoo.

"MONDAY.- As above with five Quarts of Small Beer and similarly each evening."

6. This is obviously a printer's error, for John Tyrrell, one of the prisoners from Upper Canada, returned to his homeland in 1845, where he became a cheese-maker and "a prosperous and respected citizen." He died on May 22, 1874, in his sixtieth year. See Guillet, *The Lives and Times of the Patriots,* pp. 213, 223 and note; and Prieur, *Notes d'un Condamné Politique de* 1838, p. 106 *et seq.*

7. Asa Priest, a native of Massachusetts, aged forty, "a very quiet, social man" who left a widow and three children. Gates says he died of a broken heart." See Gates's *Recollections of Life in Van Diemen's Land* (1850) for a full account of the voyage.

8. Prieur calls him «marchand banqueroutier du Haut-Canada,» appointed «Maitre d'hôtel» of the *Buffalo.*

9. Bishop Polding and the Rev. John Brady, afterwards first Roman Catholic Bishop of Perth. See Prieur, *Notes d'un Condamné Politique,* for a full account of the work of these two clergymen on behalf of the French-Canadian prisoners.

10. According to the official list, one prisoner, Benjamin Mott was a Methodist.

11. Prieur states: "The Canadian bishops had written to Monsignor Polding, and their religious and charitable messages had preceded us into these far distant regions of our harsh exile."

12. The official description of each of the prisoners is still extant in the Mitchell Library, Sydney.

13. Longbottom is a small peninsula lying between the present Concord and the Parramatta River, a little to the east of St. Luke's Park, Burwood. Three small bays which appear on modern maps of the district are named France Bay, Exile Bay and Canada Bay, apparently to commemorate the presence there of the French-Canadian prisoners. Prieur says that the clothes of all the convicts at this establishment were branded L.R, their "Croix d'honneur."

14. Henry Clinton Baddeley, whose address is given as Longbottom, according to the Register at St. John's Church, Parramatta, died 2nd March, 1842, and was buried three days later. In the *Sydney Morning Herald* of 4th June, 1842, is the application for the administration of the estate.

15. Louis Duoumouchelle, of the Parish of St. Martine, in the District of Montreal, was an innkeeper, aged 42 at the date of his arrival, a married man with six children; he was tried, on the 11th January, 1839, for treason, and, with his brother Joseph, transported for life. Ignace Gabriel Chevrefils, a farmer of the same district, aged 43, also with six children, was sentenced to transportation for life.

16. See Prieur, *Notes d'un Condamné Politique,* p. 14.6 *et seq.*, for an account of the visits of Bishop Polding and Father Brady to Longbottom.

17. John McLean, who had been Superintendent of Agriculture on Norfolk Island. He is described in *Low's Directory* for 1847 as Principal Supeintendent of Convicts, Hyde Park Barracks; private residence, Newstead House.

18. Samuel Augustus Perry, Deputy Surveyor-General under Sir Thomas Mitchell.

19. Alexander George Dumas, corresponding clerk in the : office of the Principal Superintendent of Convicts' Office, Hyde Park.

20. In 1838, Jules Joubert brought out vines from the Médoc district of France.

21. For an account of Bennelong in England, see Mackaness, *Life of Admiral Arthur Phillip,* p. 400; and Bond, *Brief Account of the Colony of Port Jackson.*

22. The population of the colony at the end of 1844 is given as 173,377, exclusive of Norfolk Island. The number of convicts in the colony is returned as 19,175, of whom upwards of 13,000 held Tickets of Leave. See *Commonwealth Historical Records,* Vol. XXIV., pp. 335-337.

23. Ducharme much exaggerates here. It is to be noted also that even as late as 1844 the number of males in the colony was twice as great as that of females.

24. Of the 58 prisoners who arrived in 1840, two died in Sydney and 55 ultimately returned to Canada. One, Joseph Marceau, son of James and Archange Marceau, a farmer of Montreal, a widower with three children, aged 34 at the date of his arrival, alone remained in New South Wales. He married in 1844 Mary Barrett, and settled at Dapto, South Coast. He died on 8th June, 1883, aged 77, leaving eleven children, one of whom, James, still survives, and many grand-children. He was buried at West Dapto Roman Catholic Cemetery, where a headstone commemorates him. His wife, Mary, died 14th February, 1909, aged 84 years. The Marceau family, which claims descent from that Francois Severin Desgraviers Marceau (1769-96), one of Napoleon's Generals who was killed while covering the French retreat at Altenkirehen, constitutes the sole remaining link of the Canadian rebels with Australia.

25. Prieur says that on the day of his departure from Sydney, in February, 1846, there still remained 13 of the original 58 in New South Wales. Prieur: *Notes d'un Condamné Politique,* p. 215.

26. Hypolite Lanctôt of St. Remi, Montreal, a notary public, aged 23, a married man with two sims, tried on 12th March and condemned to death on the 17th March, 1839.

27. John Arthur Roebuck, born at Madras in December, 1802, but brought up in Canada. M.P. for Bath, 1832, and for Sheffield, 1849-1868 and 1874-1879. A Radical, he wrote *The Colonies of England* (1849). There is a Life by R. Leader (1897).

The Buffalo.

Printed in Australia
AUHW020942290121
340425AU00004B/9

9 781922 473158